Living with Jesus TOGETHER

Bringing children into the presence of Jesus.

This material is for the children's small group meeting, ages 6-11 years.
It can be used independently or with the *Living with Jesus* series of books..

Daphne Kirk

First published in 2004 by
Daphne Kirk

Scripture references are taken from the Holy Bible, New International Version, unless otherwise stated. Copyright © 1973, 1978, 1984, by International Bible Society. Used by permission of Hodder & Stoughton Limited.

0 1 2 3 4 5 6 7 8 9

ISBN 0 9548558 0 9

Printed and bound in the United States of America

Edited and cover redesign by Lana Robison

Contact Daphne Kirk by email via her website:
www.gnation2gnation.com

To Jack and Iris,
(our parents, grandparents and great grandparents)
whose prayers for us go before the Father daily
and who have influenced children worldwide
both through their own witness and vision
and through their generations.

Using Living With Jesus Together
In A Children's Small Group Meeting

(recommended for children ages 6-11 years)

An Encounter with Jesus

Many people ask how to keep children interested, how to entertain them and have fun. However, I am rarely asked, "How do we bring children into the presence of Jesus, to have an encounter with Him?" This is the primary aim of the small group. This is what we pray and prepare for. These materials are based on the 4 W's (Welcome, Worship, Word, and Witness) providing the framework for the Holy Spirit, through prayer, to give everyone an encounter with Jesus. No matter how good the materials, they will be like wood without the fire unless there is prayer and preparation allowing the Holy Spirit to flow through them.

In these small groups, children relate to Jesus, each other and the small group leader as they welcome each other, worship Jesus together, apply the Word of God to their lives, and are equipped to win their friends for Jesus.

Welcoming Each Other

In their individual groups, the children welcome each other during refreshments (a drink and a snack), sharing together about their weeks. Encourage all the children to share, listen and respond. Respond as the children share: e.g. pray as necessary; encourage; empathize; help them carry out what they need to do.

Icebreaker

The small groups answer the icebreaker question ensuring that every child and adult has the chance to respond. Start by answering yourself to model the type and length of answer. Then go around the circle.

Worshipping Jesus

This is a time of creative worship aimed at focusing on Jesus. Begin when all the children are quiet and ready to welcome Jesus. Holding hands is a good way to bring uniformity. Use CD's or an instrument like a guitar. When music is being used as background always use instrumental music. Encourage the spiritual gifts to flow. Worship creatively: e.g. write a letter to Jesus, listen to what he is saying, listen to music, write a Psalm together.

Jesus' Word and Our Lives

This is about applying the Word of God to the lives of the children and leader. Encourage ministry whenever appropriate…child to child, adult to child, child to adult. Encourage interaction between the children, one ministering to another, one answering the questions another might have. Be ready to give your input, guiding, and training. Always facilitating the move of the Holy Spirit.

Witnessing For Jesus

This time brings the children's awareness to a lost and hurting world, but also equips and mobilizes them to make a difference and have a vision to fulfill the great commission.

And Finally!

Everyone closes with prayer, and the children are picked up by their parents from their groups.

Parents or Discipleship Time

Each week one session of the **Living With Jesus** series is identified. These discipleship books complement **Living With Jesus Together,** facilitating one-on-one relational interaction with a parent or other responsible adult. **Living With Jesus** may also be used as an extension of the small group meeting.

This week!

Suggestions for the small group leader to implement during the week:

Tips for the Children's Small Group Meeting:

- The materials are the skeleton. Keep the essence of the material, but allow the Holy Spirit to flow, sense His direction, His creativity.
- Have the children seated in a circle. Always watch the seating arrangement as this can be a deciding factor in the whole meeting!!
- Encourage the whole group to fully participate. If there is a problem, then address it: e.g. in prayer, with the child, with the parents, with those you are accountable to.
- It is important that the leader shares and takes a full part as well as the children. The leader must be able to use everyday language appropriate to the children and share at their level.
- Use a child friendly version of the Bible.
- Be well prepared: e.g. refreshments, all music on the CD player, all materials ready, etc. before the children arrive.
- Preparation will ensure that ownership is taken of the material. It is like the skeleton just waiting for the "flesh" to be put on!
- Prayer will bring the fire. It will prepare the way. But most of all, prayer will prepare the heart of the leader so that they are sensitive to the Holy Spirit.
- Use the **Living With Jesus** series as a complementary discipleship resource for parents, or as a supplement to the small group time.
- Remember that you are privileged to be part of training children who are called to reach the unreached, change the destiny of the persecuted, to be the bride of Christ, and herald the return of the King!

Table of Contents

No. 1 – Precious To Jesus

Items You Will Need	• Refreshments; music for the worship time; something precious wrapped in a parcel; a cross; 2 heart shapes for each child (two different colors); John 3:16 cut up into individual words; a watch with a second hand

Welcoming Each Other	• During this time have a drink and a snack. Clear away before beginning icebreaker. • As the children come in, encourage them to share about their week and you share about yours. Ensure that every child has the opportunity to share while everyone shows respect for the person speaking.
Icebreaker	• "Name one thing that is precious to you and why."

Worshipping Jesus	**Theme: How Precious You Are To God!** • Play a simple song about the love of Jesus. You may join in and sing, or listen to the words and think about them. • Share how you have seen the love of Jesus this week. • Spend some time thanking Jesus for His love.

Jesus' Word and Your Lives	**Theme: Precious To Jesus** • Ask the children to share their own experience of coming to know Jesus; you share your experience with them, too. • Talk about what these experiences mean to each of you today. • Show the parcel to the children and ask them to guess what is in it. Pass the parcel around. Tell the children the contents are precious to you. • When every child has held the parcel and guessed its contents, allow one child to open it. Place the contents in the middle of the group. Explain why it is so precious to you. • Read John 3:16, and ask the children to explain how precious each one of them is to Jesus. Invite each child to express how much more important they are to God than the contents of the parcel. • Spend some time talking about the impact of the Father giving His Son for people who had not even been born. • Take the cross and put it in the middle. Write your names on pieces of heart-shaped paper and place them on the cross. (Children and leader should all do this!) • Spend some time kneeling around the cross and thanking Jesus for His love.

Memory Verse Experience	• Place the individual words of John 3:16 upside down on the floor. • Divide the children into three groups. • Ask 2 groups to sit on the chairs while the third gets ready to turn the words over and place them in the right order (time them). • Do the same with the other two groups and see which group did it in the fastest time. • Say the verse together.

Witnessing for Jesus	**Theme: Naming Friends To Pray For – They Are Precious To Jesus** • Each of you, adult and children, name one of your friends who does not know Jesus. Ask why the memory verse you just learned is so important for these friends. • Take a heart of a different color and put your friend's name on it. • Place that heart on the cross and talk about how precious these friends are to Jesus. • Ask each person to place their hands on the heart of their friend and pray for them. Keep the cross for next week.
And Finally!	• Hold hands in a circle and tell Jesus how precious He is to you.

Parents or Discipleship Time	• Use the *Living With Jesus – Welcome To God's Family* workbook for children No. 1 Precious To Jesus

This week!	• Remember to pray for each member of your small group daily. • Make a list of the names in a notebook and allocate them so that they each get prayed for on a certain day. • Write down anything you hear in the spirit for each child.

No. 2 – Belonging To Jesus

<table>
<tr><td>Items You Will Need</td><td>• Refreshments; music for the worship time; passport; thin red strip; cross with the hearts on it from last week; crown</td></tr>
</table>

<table>
<tr><td>Welcoming Each Other</td><td>• During this time have a drink and a snack. Clear away before beginning icebreaker.
• As the children come in, encourage them to share about their week and you share about yours. Ensure that every child has the opportunity to share while everyone shows respect for the person speaking.</td></tr>
<tr><td>Icebreaker</td><td>• "What is your favorite place in your home and why is it special to you?"</td></tr>
</table>

<table>
<tr><td>Worshipping Jesus</td><td>Theme: God's House…And Your Place In It
• Ask two or three different children to read John 14:1-3.
• Talk about what these verses make you think about.
• Sing together about your love for Jesus.</td></tr>
</table>

<table>
<tr><td>Jesus' Word and Your Lives</td><td>Theme: Belonging To Jesus
• Each of you share which country you belong to.
• Show the children your passport and explain why you need it and what happens when you enter and leave a country.
• Explain that there are two kingdoms that God sees: the kingdom of God and the kingdom of darkness.
• Place a thin red strip as a dividing line down the center of the group.
• Select three children: two to stand on either side of the line and the third to stand on the line.
• Give one child the passport and act out moving from one country (side) to the other with the person in the middle "inspecting the passport" before allowing the child to pass over.
• Now explain that one side is the kingdom of darkness and the other is the kingdom of Light where Jesus is King.
• You, as leader, be the figure of Jesus and ask the children to try and cross from darkness to Light. Each child is to "show" you the "passport" they think will get them across. You must refuse each child until a child "shows" you the blood of Jesus!
• Read 1 John 1:7. "The Blood of Jesus cleanses us from all unrighteousness." Discuss what this means.

(continued)</td></tr>
</table>

<table>
<tr><td></td><td>

• Allow each child to come into the Kingdom of Light as they show the "passport" saying, "The Blood of Jesus has cleansed me!"
• Having all passed into the Kingdom of Light, read Luke 1:33: "He will reign forever; His Kingdom will never end."
• Share what it means to live in the Kingdom that will never end with Jesus as King.

</td></tr>
</table>

Memory Verse Experience	• Read Luke 1:33. "He will reign for ever and ever; His kingdom will never end." • Ask the children, "Who is King of the Kingdom of God?" Jesus! • Divide the group in half. • One half asks, "How long will Jesus be King?" • The other half responds, "He will reign for ever and ever; His kingdom will never end." • First half asks, "How do you know?" • Second half responds, "Luke 1:33 tells us so!" • Repeat this a few times using different combinations of groups: e.g. boys and girls; you and the children.

Witnessing for Jesus	**Theme: Jesus Is Lord!** • Show the children the cross from last week and ask them to explain what it means. (Save cross for next week.) • Place a crown on the top of the cross and explain how Jesus is the King of the lives of everyone whose name is on that cross. • Join hands and pray that Jesus will be King of the friends whose names are on the cross. • In pairs, pray that Jesus would be King of your own lives.
And Finally!	• Hold hands in a circle and tell Jesus how precious He is to you.

Parents or Discipleship Time	• Use the *Living With Jesus – Welcome To God's Family* workbook for children No. 1 Belonging To Jesus

This week!	• Remember to pray for each member of your cell daily. • Pray for Jesus to be Lord over each family represented in your small group.

No. 3 – Who Is Your Family?

Items You Will Need	• Refreshments; large sheet of paper; marker; photos of your family; cake; candles; labels; cross from the previous week

Welcoming Each Other	• During this time have a drink and a snack. Clear away before beginning icebreaker. • As the children come in, encourage them to share about their week and you share about yours. Ensure that every child has the opportunity to share while everyone shows respect for the person speaking.
Icebreaker	• "If you could choose your own name, what would you call yourself and why do you like that name?"

Worshipping Jesus	**Theme: Jesus Is Lord!** • Write on a large sheet of paper as many names for God as you can think of. These may be direct names: e.g. Jehovah Shalom, or names that His word infers – such as, "God who puts His arms around us because He loves us." • Sit quietly and read the names. • Ask each child to say which name speaks to his or her heart the most and why. • Have each person pray using the name that they have chosen (you may need to model what you mean).

Jesus' Word and Your Lives	**Theme: Becoming Part Of God's Family** • Spend some time talking about your families. (Be aware that the backgrounds of these children will be varied. Be sensitive!) • Show the children some pictures of your own family and talk about them. • Remind the children that they belong to God's kingdom. • Read Ephesians 2:19 together. Ask different children to read from their own versions. • Have them share what they think this means – especially that they belong to God's household, His family! • Talk about how you came to be part of your earthly family. (Again, be sensitive to each child's story!). • Now ask how any person can become part of God's family. Let the children explain the way of salvation! • Produce a cake with candles on it. Talk about celebrating birthdays.

(continued)

	• Light the candles (ensuring that the cake is in a safe place). Ask the children to share what they remember about when they were born into God's family. Be aware that some children may not be born again. This is an opportunity to learn about each child's spiritual life and even see some born again! • Pray together about what was said in your sharing time.

Memory Verse Experience	• Read John 14:6. "I am the way, the truth, and the life. No one comes to the Father except through Me." Say it together. • Ask one child to be "Jesus" and stand at one end, with another child being "the Father" behind him. • Ask one child to go straight to "the Father." • Stop the child and ask the group to tell them how to get to the Father (John 14:6). The child then goes to "Jesus" who takes them to the Father. • Repeat this until every child has been led to Jesus. He then leads them to the Father! Different children can play the role of the Father and Jesus.

Witnessing for Jesus	**Theme: ONLY ONE WAY TO THE FATHER** • Give each child a label. Ask them to write the name of an unsaved friend on it. • Tell them that they are identifying with this person by helping them understand what that child's life is like. • Ask each child to go to "Jesus" and ask Him to lead their friend to the Father. (Act this out as you did during the memory verse time) • When the child gets to "the Father," the child should pray and thank the Father that their friend will one day come to Him. • Ask "Jesus" to hold the cross from previous weeks and take that cross to the Father. • Ask "Jesus" to repeat John 14:6.
And Finally!	• Hold hands in a circle and tell Jesus how precious He is to you.

Parents or Discipleship Time	• Use the *Living With Jesus – Welcome To God's Family* workbook for children No. 3 – Who Is Your Family?

This week!	• Remember to pray for each member of your group daily. • Choose two children this week and find out what they need prayer for (by asking them) and pray for them. Call them during the week and say that you prayed for them. Repeat this each week until every child has been prayed for and contacted.

No. 4 – Caring In The Family

Items You Will Need	• Refreshments; music for the worship time; different items of food (see the Word time); paper and pens; cross from the previous week; globe or map

Welcoming Each Other	• During this time have a drink and a snack. Clear away before beginning icebreaker. • As the children come in, encourage them to share about their week and you share about yours. Ensure that every child has the opportunity to share while everyone shows respect for the person speaking.
Icebreaker	• "What is your favorite food and what is the food you hate most? Why is this?"

Worshipping Jesus	**Theme: The Bread Of Life** • Stand and sing a praise song. • Sing a worship song kneeling. • As the worship song is repeated, ask any children who need prayer to stand in the middle. Let the other children lay hands on them. Everyone pray for them together. • Sing the worship song again.

Jesus' Word and Your Lives	**Theme: How do You Grow Strong As Christians?** • Have different items of food (some that are healthy and some that are not). • Ask the children to place them into two piles: One that is good for their body and another that is not. • Then show them some baby food, milk in baby bottles, etc. • Ask the children if they still eat baby food. If they say no, ask them why. • Read Hebrews 5:12. "Milk is for beginners, inexperienced in God's ways; solid food is for the mature." • Discuss what this means, emphasize that you need to have the right food for the right stage of life, and the right people to give you what you need. • Talk about being born into God's family as a baby in Jesus and how a new Christian grows. • Put some small pieces of paper in the middle. Ask the children to write (or draw) things that will help them grow as Christians. Then write things that will keep them from growing into Jesus' image. • Now place these notes either in the "good for you" food pile: e.g. the Bible; meeting with other Christians; witnessing for Jesus, or the "bad for you" food pile: e.g. some TV programs; harmful talk. *(continued)*

	•Now ask the children to think of things they particularly need as baby Christians and put those with the baby foods: e.g. helping to pray; remembering the Bible. •Finally, encourage the children to share what they think they are "eating" as Christians that is "bad food" for them and how they can stop "eating" it. Then encourage them to share what they are "eating" that is "good food" for them. •Pray together in these areas.
Memory Verse Experience	•Read John 14:27. "Peace I leave with you; my peace I give you… Do not let your hearts be troubled and do not be afraid." •Stand in pairs. Have one child portray Jesus and say the verse to the other child, then have them change over and repeat. •In pairs, share one thing that troubles them or makes them afraid. Pray for each other and say the verse together several times.
Witnessing for Jesus	**Theme: Praying For Peace In The World** •Pray in pairs for their unsaved friends. •Keep the cross from the previous weeks with the names on it as a focus. •Have a picture of the world or a globe and share about why the world needs Jesus' peace. •Lay your hands on the globe/map and speak John 14:27 over it. Pray into the areas that have been talked about.
And Finally!	•Hold hands in a circle; sing an appropriate song and pray for the coming week.
Parents or Discipleship Time	•Use the *Living With Jesus – Welcome To God's Family* workbook for children No. 4 – Caring In The Family
This week!	•Remember to pray for each member of your cell daily. •Continue to choose children this week and find out what they need prayer for (by asking them) and pray for them. Call them during the week and say that you prayed for them. Repeat this each week until every child has been prayed for and contacted.

No. 5 – Your New Body

Items You Will Need	• Refreshments; music for worship time; pencils and paper for each child (and adult!); drawn outline of a body; memory verse cut up; cross from previous week

Welcoming Each Other	• During this time have a drink and a snack. Clear away before beginning icebreaker. • As the children come in, encourage them to share about their week and you share about yours. Ensure that every child has the opportunity to share while everyone shows respect for the person speaking.
Icebreaker	• "Tell something that you really like (or appreciate) about the person on your right. Why are they important to you?"

Worshipping Jesus	**Theme: Appreciating God** • Take turns saying something you really appreciate about God. • Thank God for all the things you appreciate about Him. • Play some quiet music and get into pairs. Thank Jesus for each other – pray for your small group. • Sing a song of praise standing and lifting your hands to Him.

Jesus' Word and Your Lives	**Theme: Members Of The Body** • Each of you draw a picture of a person, but put all the body parts in the wrong place: e.g. the leg where the head should be! • Talk about the implications of having a body like this!! • Talk about Jesus sitting at the right hand of God in heaven and the fact that you are His Body on the earth until He returns. • Read 1 Corinthians 12:18 and share what you think it means. • Now share about how God made your small group a part of His Body. • Ask each child to think for a moment, then give them a piece of paper and ask them to finish the sentence, "I am like Jesus' (name a body part)… because I…". For example, "I am like Jesus' feet because I go to the places He wants me to go," or "I am like Jesus' mouth because I tell others about Him." They can write more than one Body part, but each one needs to be written on a separate piece of paper! • Take the drawn outline of a body, put it on the floor and stick the papers over the appropriate body parts. If some parts are not identified, more can be added. • Talk about how important each part is. Refer back to the original drawings to see how Jesus' body needs each part in the right place, too! • Read 1 Corinthians 12:18-21 and discuss it with each other.

Memory Verse Experience	• Say 1 Corinthians 12:18 together. "But in fact God has arranged the parts in the body, every one of them, just as he wanted them to be." • Have the words on different pieces of paper. Put them in the wrong order and ask the group to say it. • Ask the children to arrange them in proper order (just as the Body needs to be arranged properly!). • Repeat the verse. • Pray in groups of three. Each group choose one piece of paper off the Body (I am like Jesus' hands because…) and pray for each other to truly live that out.

Witnessing for Jesus	**Theme: Showing Jesus' Love** • Put the cross from the previous week with the names of friends who don't know Jesus in the middle. • Instruct each child to take one name. Ask them to imagine how they could show the love of Jesus to a friend: e.g. being kind; helping them. • Pray together about these ideas. • Tell the group that next week you will all share what happened when they put these ideas into action.
And Finally!	• Hold hands in a circle. Thank Jesus that you are His Body and that you are going to show Him to everyone you meet this week.

Parents or Discipleship Time	• Use the *Living With Jesus – Welcome To God's Family* workbook for children No. 5 – Your New Body

This week!	• Remember to pray for each member of your cell daily. • Continue to choose children this week and find out what they need prayer for (by asking them) and pray for them. Call them during the week and say that you prayed for them. Repeat this each week until every child has been prayed for and contacted.

No. 6 – Growing Up In Your Family

Items You Will Need	• Refreshments; music for the worship time; a sword with "Word of God" written on it; concordance; cross from the previous weeks

Welcoming Each Other	• During this time have a drink and a snack. Clear away before beginning icebreaker. • As the children come in, encourage them to share about their week and you share about yours. Ensure that every child has the opportunity to share while everyone shows respect for the person speaking.
Icebreaker	• "Name one thing that you did that was naughty. What happened as a result?"

Worshipping Jesus	**Theme: How Can You Praise God?** • Read Psalm 66:1-5 and ask each person to read a verse (the Psalm may be read more than once!). • How many ways does the verse say that they can respond to God? e.g. shout, sing, say, come, see. • Take one or two of these expressions and lead the children in praise to Jesus.

Jesus' Word and Your Lives	**Theme: Using The Word Of God As The Sword**
	• Have a contest between the children to see who is the strongest. (Arm wrestling is one idea!) Strength helps us fight!
	• Now ask how they can be tested to know if they are strong for Jesus! Examples: how they stand against temptation, how they react when wronged, etc.
	• Share things that help them be strong for Jesus: e.g. prayer, the Word, and wearing the armor to protect us...dead soldiers can't fight!.
	• Read Ephesians 6:17.
	• Having already prepared a sword with "The Word of God" written on it, talk about how Jesus used the Word to fight off Satan when he was tempted. Matthew 4:1-11
	• Ask the children if they can remember how they have used God's Word as a sword from previous memory verses they have learned.
	    1. When they are afraid. John 14:27
	    2. When someone says there are many ways to God. John 14:6
	    3. When people say Jesus is dead. Luke 1:33
	
	(continued)

<table>
<tr><td></td><td>•Now ask the children what situations make it hard for them to "fight Satan" and help them find some verses to give them strength (you can teach them how to use a concordance at this point if they are old enough).
•Let the child copy out their verse. Pray for each other in these areas and confess that Scripture as the child is prayed for.</td></tr>
</table>

<table>
<tr><td>Memory Verse Experience</td><td>•Read Ephesians 6:17.
•Ask the children to separate into pairs and act out the verse as they say it.
•Let each pair show the others what skit they made. Let the entire group join in the second time.</td></tr>
</table>

<table>
<tr><td>Witnessing for Jesus</td><td>Theme: Jesus Has Won The Battle
•Share about what happened when each person showed the love of Jesus to a friend (as discussed last week).
•Talk about the battle that is being waged for their friends. Satan wants them, but Jesus died for them.
•Bring the cross from the previous week into the middle of the group.
•Talk about how the battle was won when Jesus died and rose again.
•Stand in a circle around the cross and spend some time thanking, clapping, and cheering because the battle has already been won for these people to come to Jesus.</td></tr>
<tr><td>And Finally!</td><td>•Hold hands in a circle and sing a song of praise. Then hold hands in pairs and pray for each other and the coming week.</td></tr>
</table>

<table>
<tr><td>Parents or Discipleship Time</td><td>•Use the Living With Jesus – Welcome To God's Family workbook for children No. 6 – Growing Up In Your Family</td></tr>
</table>

<table>
<tr><td>This week!</td><td>•Remember to pray for each member of your cell daily.
•Continue to choose children this week and find out what they need prayer for (by asking them) and pray for them. Call them in the week and say that you prayed for them. Repeat this each week until every child has been prayed for and contacted.</td></tr>
</table>

No. 1 – Baptism

Items You Will Need	• Refreshments; read *"When A Child Asks To Be Baptized"* by Daphne Kirk and/or look carefully at the diagrams from *"Living With Jesus - Special Times and Gifts"*; quiet worship music; large sheet of paper; paper and pencil for each member of the small group; memory verse written out with the word "we" missing

Welcoming Each Other	• During this time have a drink and a snack. Clear away before beginning icebreaker. • As the children come in, encourage them to share about their week and you share about yours. Ensure that every child has the opportunity to share while everyone shows respect for the person speaking.
Icebreaker	• "Tell about one moment in your life that was very special to you. Why was it so special?"

Worshipping Jesus	**Theme: Worshipping & Listening** • Play a quiet worship song – ask the children to kneel and let Jesus speak to them through the song as they listen. • Ask them what they heard Jesus say to them. • Stand and sing the worship song together. • As the music continues to play, ask any child who needs prayer to stand in the middle and direct the whole group to pray for them.

Jesus' Word and Your Lives	**Theme: What Is Baptism?** • Spend some time talking about baptism in your church. Let the children share what they had seen, what had happened, what they thought about it, etc. • Draw the picture of the baptismal pool. (Diagram 1 from *Living With Jesus – Special Times & Gifts*) • Ask the children what happens when someone goes into the water. (Draw the arrows shown on the diagram.) • Talk about Jesus' death, burial and resurrection. • Draw diagram 2 from *Living With Jesus – Special Times & Gifts*. • Read Romans 6:4 from several versions that you have. • Ask what the verse means. • Now draw diagram 3 showing how pictures 1 and 2 come together, and we call it baptism. (continued)

<table>
<tr><td></td><td>
• Share with them your church's policy on children and Baptism.
• Let the children do these three diagrams in pairs. Have them talk to each other about what the pictures mean.
• In pairs, pray for someone who the children have seen baptized. First share together how you could pray for them.
</td></tr>
</table>

Memory Verse Experience	• Find and read Romans 6:4. "Just as Jesus was raised from the dead through the glory of the Father so we too may live a new life." • Share together what you think this means. • Now show the children the verse written out with the word "we" missing. Each child should read it and put their name in the blank space. • In pairs repeat the verse putting the other person's name in the space. • Pray together thanking Jesus for the new life that you have because of Him.

Witnessing for Jesus	**Theme: Praying For Schools** • Talk about life in the children's schools. Encourage them to share joys and problems. • Stand in a circle and put a chair in the middle. Have each child pray for the things they just shared.
And Finally!	• Hold hands in a circle and pray for the entire group as they prepare to be in their schools and homes this week. Thank Jesus that He is there with them.

Parents or Discipleship Time	• Use the *Living With Jesus – Special Times & Gifts* workbook for children No. 1 – Baptism

This week!	• Continue to pray for the children in their schools. • Follow up on the things they shared. • Call them and encourage them in the week.

Baptism

There are some very special times you will share together.

Read Mark 1:9-11

He b _ _ _ _ _ _ _ Him.

Baptism is when someone who is following Jesus goes into the water,
right under it and then comes up again.

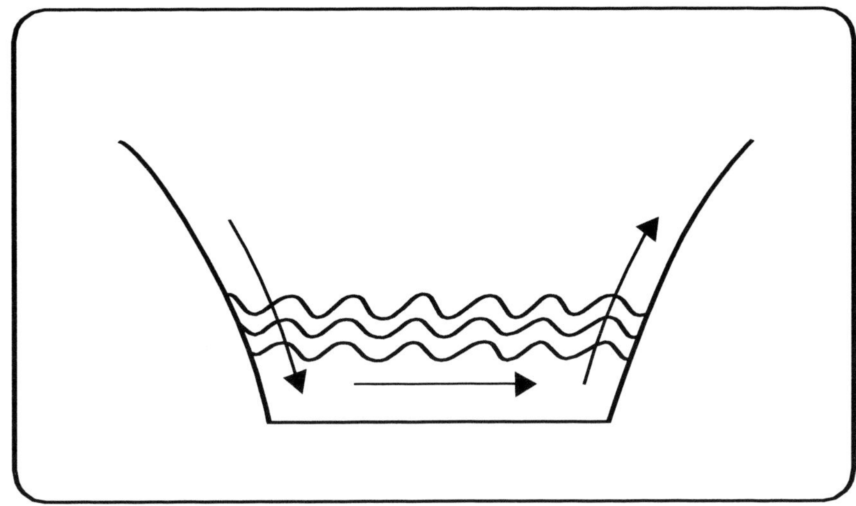

Jesus died on the cross, was buried in the grave and came alive again.

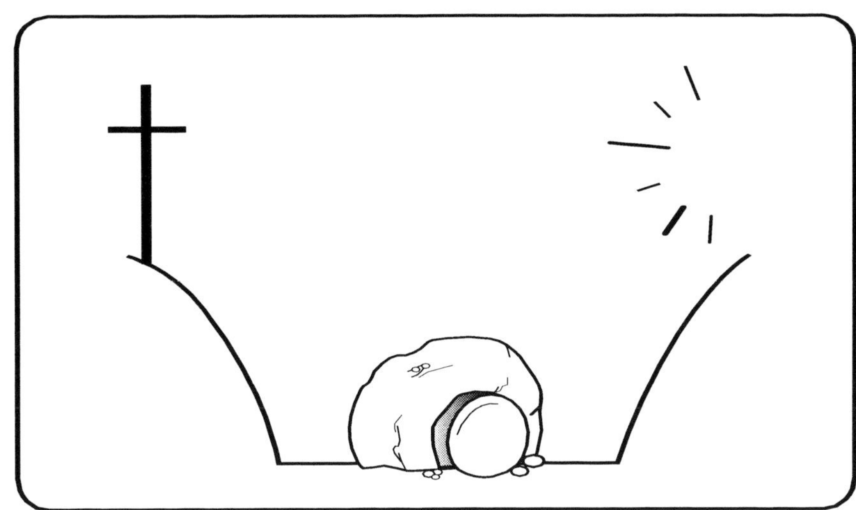

Also read *When a Child Asks to be Baptized* by Daphne Kirk

So we show that our old life is dead and buried and that we have a new life in the Kingdom of God.

Being baptized is really important.
It is something Jesus did and something He told us to do.

Now read Romans 6:4

We were therefore _ _ _ _ _ _ with

Him through baptism into _ _ _ _ _

in order that, just as _ _ _ _ _ _ was

raised from the dead through the

glory of the _ _ _ _ _ _ , we too may

live a _ _ _ _ _ _ _ .

Do you understand these verses? . . .

If you said 'No', your special friend will help you.

No. 2 – The Lord's Supper

Items You Will Need	• Refreshments; read *"When A Child Asks To Take Communion"* by Daphne Kirk; music for the worship time; small table with a large piece of bread and some wine/juice on it; a picture of one of the schools the children attend, paper, envelope and pencils

Welcoming Each Other	• During this time have a drink and a snack. Clear away before beginning icebreaker. • As the children come in, encourage them to share about their week and you share about yours. Ensure that every child has the opportunity to share while everyone shows respect for the person speaking.
Icebreaker	• "What was the best party that you ever went to, and why was it so fun?"

Worshipping Jesus	**Theme: Giving Jesus Honor** • Begin with a worship song. • Ask one or two children to read Revelation 4:11. • Talk about what it means to give Jesus "honor." Apply this to life at home, school, as well as when you are together in your small group. • Ask each child to complete the following sentence, "I honor you, Jesus because you are…" • Stand and sing a song of praise.

Jesus' Word and Your Lives	**Theme: Jesus' Last Meal** • Talk again about the special parties the children have attended. Focus on the atmosphere: e.g. happy/noisy • Place the table in the center of the room. Put the bread and wine in the middle as a focal point. • Read Matthew 26:26-36 and talk about what was happening. Ask them how they think the disciples must have felt, what the atmosphere would have been like, what Jesus might have been feeling, etc. • Read it again and let the children act it out. • Tell them that this was Jesus' special meal; His last one on this earth with His disciples. • Share together about what happens when communion is taken in your church and explain what the church teaches about children taking communion. • Talk about times of communion the children have been in and let them share what it was like for them.

(continued)

	• Go around the circle and thank Jesus for inviting you to this special meal with Him. • Ask the children to lay their hand on the table where the bread and wine are and joyfully thank Jesus for giving you this special life with Him because of His death.

Memory Verse Experience	• Pick up the bread, break it and say "The Lord Jesus took bread...broke it and said, "This is my body which is given for you. Do this in remembrance of Me." 1 Corinthians 11:23-24. • Ask all the children to say the verse after you. • Now ask each child to get up, break the bread, and say the verse together as they do it.

Witnessing for Jesus	**Theme: Praying For The Teachers** • Bring a brochure/picture of one of the schools the children attend. • Talk about the teachers. • Ask each child to take one teacher and pray for them. • Give each child a piece of paper and an envelope. Let them write a few lines telling the teacher that they prayed for them. • Together hold the letters and pray for the teachers who will receive the letters. • Ensure that the letters get to each teacher this week.
And Finally!	• Stand in a circle, put the letters in the middle, and sing a song of praise over them before praying together.

Parents or Discipleship Time	• Use the *Living With Jesus – Staying Protected* workbook for children No. 1 Fighting in God's Army

This week!	• Pray a scripture over each child and family represented. • Ensure that the letters get to each teacher this week.

No. 3 – Being Filled With The Spirit

Items You Will Need	• Refreshments; music for the worship time; basket of fruit; one fruit labeled (see Word time); fruit cut out of paper for each child; pencils; "tree" to put the fruit on; quiet worship music (instrumental only); music or a recording of any song that lists the fruit of the Spirit; large thank you card

Welcoming Each Other	• During this time have a drink and a snack. Clear away before beginning icebreaker. • As the children come in, encourage them to share about their week and you share about yours. Ensure that every child has the opportunity to share while everyone shows respect for the person speaking.
Icebreaker	• "If you were a piece of fruit which one would you be and why?"

Worshipping Jesus	**Theme: Jesus In The Center** • If you know a song about the fruit of the Spirit, sing it together; otherwise, sing a praise song. • Hold hands and pray for the person on the left - then pray for the person on the right. (Everyone do this at the same time!) • Now imagine Jesus in the centre of the circle – go around the circle and ask each person to say what he/she would like to say to Jesus. • Sing a worship song.

Jesus' Word and Your Lives	**Theme: The Fruit Of The Spirit** • Talk about trees and the fruit they bear. How the fruit identifies the tree, how it shows how healthy the tree is, how it is not just for the tree, but for people to eat, etc. • Show the basket of fruit with one piece of fruit with a label on it naming a fruit of the Spirit. • Give each child one of the unlabeled fruits, and if appropriate, allow them to eat it. Leave the one labeled fruit in the basket. • Read Galatians 5:22 and 23. • Ask them why the fruit in the basket is different. Let them read the labels and talk about this as fruit that Jesus gives us from the Holy Spirit. • Share about why the Spirit's fruit lasts forever and cannot disappear even when you give it away to others. • Give each child a fruit cut out of paper and let them write the names of the fruit of the Spirit on it.

(continued)

<table>
<tr><td></td><td>
<ul>
<li>Put the "paper fruit" on the tree that you made beforehand.</li>
<li>Ask each child to think carefully about which fruit they need to see more of in their lives.</li>
<li>Explain that the fruit is a gift from the Holy Spirit.</li>
<li>Ask the children to lie on the floor and lay their hands on themselves. Play some quiet music and let them "see" and experience the Holy Spirit washing over them.</li>
<li>Ask the children to share what they experienced lying there.</li>
<li>Now ask them to thank Him for the gifts of this fruit in their lives.</li>
</ul>
</td></tr>
</table>

Memory Verse Experience

- Read Galatians 5:23. "The fruit of the Spirit is love, joy, peace, patience, kindness, goodness, faithfulness, gentleness and self control."
- Stand in a circle with the fruit basket in the middle and let each child name one aspect of the fruit: e.g. joy/peace
- Say together "The fruit of the Spirit is …" then go around the circle with each child saying their particular fruit.
- Let the children change places and see if they can say their fruit in the right order. Repeat this.
- Ask one child to stand in the middle holding the basket and have everyone else clap for the gift of the Holy Spirit who gives the wonderful fruit.

Witnessing for Jesus

And Finally!

Theme: Praying For The Fire Brigade
- Report what happened when the letters were given to the teachers.
- Pray for those teachers again.
- Talk about the fire brigade in your area… and what their lives must be like.
- Ask each child to write a line on the thank you card for the fire brigade.
- Pass the card around and have each pray for the fire brigade while holding the card.
- Kneel and ask each child to pray that in the coming week the fruit of the Spirit will be seen in their lives.

Parents or Discipleship Time

- Use the *Living With Jesus – Special Times & Gifts* workbook for children No. 3 – Being Filled With The Spirit

This week!

- Pray for each child (and yourself) to have the fruit growing healthily in your lives and also for the fruit of the Spirit to be shown in every family.
- Ensure the thank you card gets to the fire brigade this week.

No. 4 – More Gifts

Items You Will Need	• Refreshments; worship music; container; small pieces of paper and pencils; parcel as described in the Word section; envelope with memory verse (see the Memory Verse Experience section)

Welcoming Each Other	• During this time have a drink and a snack. Clear away before beginning icebreaker. • As the children come in, encourage them to share about their week and you share about yours. Ensure that every child has the opportunity to share while everyone shows respect for the person speaking.
Icebreaker	• "What is the best gift you have ever received and why was it so special to you?"

Worshipping Jesus	**Theme: What Jesus Has Done** • Talk together about the different things you have received from Jesus this week. As each person shares some great things Jesus has done for them, ask them to thank Him. • Give each child a piece of paper to write a short thank you note to Jesus. • Ask if one or two would be willing to read what they wrote. • Place the notes in a container and sing a praise song as it is passed around the group. • One person pray a prayer of thanks while holding the basket.

Jesus' Word and Your Lives	**Theme: More Gifts** • Place a wrapped parcel in the middle. Don't let them open it yet. • Explain that the Holy Spirit has many gifts He is ready to give you. • Read 1 Corinthians 12:7-11 using a child's version of the Bible. • Read it a second time and ask the children to count how many gifts are in the verses. • Ask one child to open only the first layer of the parcel. They will find that the second layer has LOVE written all over it. • Spend some time talking about the importance of every gift being wrapped up in love. • Then ask another child to open the final layer of the parcel where they will find the words of one gift that you have chosen. • This is an opportunity for you to tell them stories of when you have seen that gift used, to let the children share if they have seen it used and to answer their questions. Choose a gift that you are most familiar with.

(continued)

| | • Finally, ask them what would happen if that gift was used without being wrapped up in love.
• Give them two scenarios of what could happen: 1. When the gift is used in love, and 2. when it might be used with pride.
• Pray in pairs that everything you do will be wrapped up in Jesus' love.
• Talk about the fact that gifts are given because you love someone. Jesus loves you so much that He wants to give you gifts.
• Look at John 3:16 together to find the greatest gift that God gave you. Thank Him for that gift! |

| **Memory Verse Experience** | • Read 1 Corinthians 13:13. "These three: faith, hope and love. But the greatest of these is love."
• Ask everyone why they think love is the greatest: e.g. because that's who Jesus is; no one gets hurt; they are concerned about the other person instead of themselves.
• Divide into groups of three. Give an envelope filled with the words of the memory verse. Ask them to place the words in the right order.
• Say the verse again together. |

| **Witnessing for Jesus** | **Theme: Praying For The Police**
• Remind the children that you have prayed for schools and the fire brigade. Report what happened when the card was taken to the fire brigade last week.
• Tell them that this week it is the Police you will be praying for!
• Talk about the Police and the work they do and what must it be like being a Police Officer.
• Write a short note in a card: each child complete the line "Thank you for………."
• Ask one child to stand in the middle of the group holding the card while everyone else puts their hands on that person and prays for the Police. |
| **And Finally!** | • Stand in threes and pray protection over each other this week |

| **Parents or Discipleship Time** | • Use the *Living With Jesus – Special Times & Gifts* workbook for children No. 4 – More Gifts |

| **This week!** | • Continue to pray protection over every family of the children in your small group.
• Ensure the Police receive the card this week. |

No. 5 – The Spirit's Power

Items You Will Need	•Read Acts 2:17-18 as a preparation for today. Refreshments; an identically wrapped gift for each child; card for the ambulance service; large sheet of paper; marker for writing

Welcoming Each Other	•During this time have a drink and a snack. Clear away before beginning icebreaker. •As the children come in, encourage them to share about their week and you share about yours. Ensure that every child has the opportunity to share while everyone shows respect for the person speaking.
Icebreaker	•"What is the most powerful thing you have ever seen, and what was happening when you saw it?"

Worshipping Jesus	**Theme: Powerful God** •Show the children some pictures that show the power of God in creation: e.g. waterfall, ocean. •Talk about these pictures and ask them what the pictures reveal about God. •Write a short poem together on a large sheet of paper, where each line starts "God's power is amazing. I know because…" •Read the poem together.

Jesus' Word and Your Lives	**Theme: The Spirit's Power** •Give each child a small gift wrapped up. Tell them not to open it. •Now tell each child that they have to give their gift to another child. Ask them how they feel about that! •Then, make sure that each one gives and receives a gift from another member of the group. Let them open their gift! •Now ask them what the experience was like. •Explain that the gifts Jesus gives them are to be given away like this. Each one giving and each one receiving. •Tell the children that He gives them His power to serve others and share together how they can do that. •Tell them that the fruit of the Spirit (See if they remember what it is!) is to bring happiness to others. •The gifts from the Holy Spirit are for giving to others. Talk together about these things.

(continued)

- Now ask the children if any of them have ever prayed and asked the Holy Spirit to really fill them with His power. If they have, let them share about the experience and if they spoke in tongues afterwards.
- Read Acts 2:17. "I will pour out my Spirit on all people." Ask if that includes children!
- Ask the children to lie on the floor and listen again as the Holy Spirit pours Himself all over them.
- Go round and ask the Holy Spirit to fill each child as you lay hands on them.
- Then let the whole group pray quietly in tongues. (Children will get their own breakthrough at this time. It does not matter if the children pretend.)
- Then sing a song of praise.

Memory Verse Experience	- Read 1 Corinthians 14:1. "Follow the way of love and eagerly desire the spiritual gifts." - Say to the children, "What do we follow?" They repeat, "the way of love." - "What do we desire?" They say, "The spiritual gifts." - "Where does the Bible tell us this?" They say, "1 Corinthians 14:1. - Do this several times; the children can ask the question too!

Witnessing for Jesus	**Theme: Praying For The Ambulance Service** - Report on the card taken to the Police. - Remind them that you have prayed for schools, Fire brigade, Police…and now…the ambulance service. - Share what it might be like to be in the ambulance service. - Stand, hold hands, and pray for the ambulance service. - Ask each child to write a line in the card saying, "I prayed for you because…" - Take the card to them this week.
And Finally!	- Hold hands in a circle and sing a song of praise. Then hold hands in pairs and pray for each other and the coming week.

Parents or Discipleship Time	- Use the *Living With Jesus – Special Times & Gifts* workbook for children No. 5 The Spirit's Power

This week!	- Pray that each child and each family really experiences the power of the Holy Spirit. - Ensure the card gets to the ambulance service this week.

No. 1 – Talking & Listening

<table>
<tr><td>Items You Will Need</td><td>• Refreshments; music for the worship time; small notebook for each child; pencils; instrumental worship music; pictures of people from different nations</td></tr>
</table>

<table>
<tr><td>Welcoming Each Other</td><td>• During this time have a drink and a snack. Clear away before beginning icebreaker.
• As the children come in, encourage them to share about their week and you share about yours. Ensure that every child has the opportunity to share while everyone shows respect for the person speaking.</td></tr>
<tr><td>Icebreaker</td><td>• In pairs, at the same time – tell each other about your favorite TV program. It might help to count to three so that they all start together. Then, one at a time, try and repeat what the other person said!
• Repeat the experience, but this time, one talks, the other listens and then repeats.</td></tr>
</table>

<table>
<tr><td>Worshipping Jesus</td><td>Theme: Thanking God For His People
• Sing a praise song together, (encouraging the children to clap, etc.) really expressing your praise to Him.
• Share together about people who have helped you to know Jesus better.
• Thank Jesus for them and pray for them.
• Sing a song of thanks to Him.</td></tr>
</table>

<table>
<tr><td>Jesus' Word and
Your Lives</td><td>Theme: Listening To Jesus & Hearing His Voice
• Discuss the icebreaker. Why was it difficult to repeat something that they were not listening to? Why was it easier when they listened to each other?
• Spend some time discussing what happens if you only talk to Jesus, but never listen to Him.
• Read 1 Samuel 3:2-11.
• Ask two of the children to act it out as another child reads it again.
• Ask the children if they have ever heard Jesus speak to them. Encourage them to tell how, when, what He said, and what they did with what they heard.
• Discuss the story of Samuel. He was a child, he needed help, and he believed that it was God speaking to him.
• Let the children know that Jesus still speaks today and wants to speak to them, so they need to listen.</td></tr>
</table>

(continued)

	• Ask the children to lie on the floor with their eyes closed, while you play some quiet instrumental (without words) worship music. Tell them that Jesus will speak into their hearts as they lie there. Pray, asking the Holy Spirit to speak to each child. Play the music softly while everyone is very quiet. • Ask the children to write or draw in their small "Listening To Jesus" notebooks what they heard or saw. • Share these things together, affirming each child.

Memory Verse Experience	• Ask everyone to read Galatians 2:20. "Christ lives in me… I live by faith in the Son of God." • Ask the children where Jesus is. ("In me!") Because He is in you, it is, therefore, simple to hear Him. • Ask the group to sit. One half stands and says, "Christ lives in me," the other half stands and says, "I live by faith in the Son of God." Everyone sit and say Galatians 2:20 together. • Repeat this a few times. • Then ask: "Where does Jesus live?" ("In me!") • "How do you live?" ("By faith in the Son of God!")

Witnessing for Jesus	**Theme: The Nations** • Read Psalm 2:8. "I will make the nations your inheritance, the ends of the earth your possession." • Discuss what you think this verse means. Help them to understand that the nations belong to Jesus. • Show them pictures of people from different nations. • Talk about which nations any of them have visited and ask them to tell what these countries were like. • Impress on them the love of Jesus for each of these nations. • Ask each child that shared about a nation to pray for that country.
And Finally!	• Stand in a circle, have everyone turn to the right, and tell the children to place their hands on the shoulders of the person in front of them. Have them pray for that person. Then let them turn around and do the same for the child on the other side.

Parents or Discipleship Time	• Use the *Living With Jesus – Talking & Listening* workbook for children No. 1 – Talking & Listening

This week!	• Continue to pray for the children in their schools. Follow up on the things they shared in the group. Call them and encourage them in the week.

No. 2 – Who Is Important?

<table>
<tr><td>Items You Will Need</td><td>•Refreshments; worship music; "Listening To Jesus" notebooks from last week; pencils. Map, pictures and information about an unreached people (check out sites like www.linkingup.com, www.persecution.com)</td></tr>
</table>

<table>
<tr><td>Welcoming Each Other</td><td>•During this time have a drink and a snack. Clear away before beginning icebreaker.
•As the children come in, encourage them to share about their week and you share about yours. Ensure that every child has the opportunity to share while everyone shows respect for the person speaking.</td></tr>
<tr><td>Icebreaker</td><td>•"Name someone who is very important to you, and say why."</td></tr>
</table>

<table>
<tr><td>Worshipping Jesus</td><td>Theme: Freedom In Worship
•Share with one another about the freedom you have to worship Jesus. Talk to them about some of the nations that don't have that freedom.
•Thank Jesus for the freedom you have to worship Him together.
•Spend some time in praise and worship as you appreciate that privilege.</td></tr>
</table>

<table>
<tr><td>Jesus' Word and Your Lives</td><td>Theme: A Quiet Place To Listen To Jesus
•Ask the children when and where they pray. Encourage them to share the places that they find it easiest to pray. You share your experiences too.
•Help them to understand that they can pray anywhere, but sometimes people have a favorite place.
•Read Luke 5:16 and ask where Jesus went to pray. How important was it for Him to talk to His Father?
•Ask the group to kneel down and close their eyes.
•In the silence, ask the children to pretend that they are on a quiet lonely mountain. The only other person there with them is Jesus, who is right beside them.
•Tell the children to be very quiet as they listen to what Jesus says as they kneel on that mountain together.
•Let the children write in their notebooks what Jesus tells them.
•Share these things together. You share what you heard, as well.
•Now ask the children to close their eyes again and this time they will reply to what Jesus said.
•They can write this in their books also and share them together.</td></tr>
</table>

| **Memory Verse Experience** | •Ask the children who or what they think Jesus prayed about.
•Ask a child to read John 17:20-21. "I pray for those who will believe in me... that all of them may be one."
•Discuss who He was praying for (everyone today), and consider the wonder of Jesus praying for them 2000 years before they were even born.
•Ask each child to read John 17:20-21 from their Bible. Then ask who can say it without looking! |

| **Witnessing for Jesus** | **Theme: Praying For The Nations**
•Read Psalm 2:8. "I will make the nations your inheritance, the ends of the earth your possession."
•Ask the children how many times they have heard about Jesus, how many churches there are where you live, what other ways they can hear about Jesus!
•Talk with the children about the fact that there are people on this earth who have never had the opportunity of hearing about Jesus once.
•Talk about how easy, or not so easy, it is to find out about Jesus.
•Take the map and identify some of the nations where there are so many who have never heard of Him.
•Talk about one of these nations and show pictures.
•Lay hands on the map and pray for the nation you have chosen. |
| **And Finally!** | •Pray together that you will set time aside to "listen" to Jesus. |

| **Parents or Discipleship Time** | •Use the *Living With Jesus – Talking & Listening* workbook for children No. 2 – Who Is Important? |

| **This week!** | •Pray that the children will have a lifestyle of hearing the voice of their Father. |

No. 3 – Checking It Out!

<table>
<tr><td>Items You Will Need</td><td>•Refreshments; "Listening To Jesus" notebooks; pencils; quiet music; 2 puzzles; check out the website www.linkingup.com, paper; envelopes and addresses of the embassies of nations where there are persecuted Christians</td></tr>
</table>

<table>
<tr><td>Welcoming Each Other</td><td>•During this time have a drink and a snack. Clear away before beginning icebreaker.
•As the children come in, encourage them to share about their week and you share about yours. Ensure that every child has the opportunity to share while everyone shows respect for the person speaking.</td></tr>
<tr><td>Icebreaker</td><td>•"What is your favorite book, and why do you enjoy it?"</td></tr>
</table>

<table>
<tr><td>Worshipping Jesus</td><td>Theme: Hearing Jesus In Your Worship
•Sing a praise song together.
•Play some quiet music with no words – let the children sit quietly and then share what Jesus said to them as the music was playing.
•Sing a worship song together as each person decides if they want to sit, kneel, stand, etc. Encourage them to make their own decision on this.</td></tr>
</table>

<table>
<tr><td>Jesus' Word and Your Lives</td><td>Theme: Checking Thing out Against The Word
•Take a simple puzzle and ask the group you put it together – give them no instructions or picture at all.
•Then give them a puzzle of the same difficulty and ask them to put it together, but this time give them the picture.
•Share together about the importance of checking things out so that they know everything is O.K.
•Talk about the Bible and how to check things out there.
•Ask each child and adult to read one thing out of their "Listening To Jesus" notebook that Jesus said to them, and ask the others if it agrees with the Bible. Stress the importance of checking what you hear against the Bible so that you can be sure it is the voice of Jesus.
•Play some quiet music and ask the Holy Spirit to give each child a picture, which they can draw in their notebooks.
•In groups of three, look at the pictures and share what they think Jesus might be saying to them through that picture.</td></tr>
</table>

Memory Verse Experience	•Read Psalm 119:105. "Your Word is a lamp to my feet and a light for my path." •Talk together about how light or lamps show you the way. Discuss what would happen if it was totally dark with no light at all. •The Bible helps you to see the way. •Ask the group to walk around in a circle and say the Scripture out loud together. Every time they say "feet", they stamp the ground. When they say "path", they touch the ground! •Go around the group and let each person say one thing that the Bible agrees with: e.g. Jesus loves me; Jesus says He will never leave me; etc. •Then go around saying one thing that the Bible does not say: e.g. You must have a red car; it is OK to be a little naughty; etc. •Stress again the importance of the Bible in helping you know the right way and read Psalm 119:105 again.

| **Witnessing for Jesus** | **Theme: The Nations**
•Read Psalm 2:8. "I will make the nations your inheritance, the ends of the earth your possession."
•Remind the children about the people who have never had an opportunity to hear about Jesus and talk about it again for a while.
•Having checked out the website www.linkingup.com (a website for children, about persecuted nations) share with them some of what you learned, especially "kids of courage"! Talk together to inspire them to make a difference but not to frighten them!
•Let them each write a letter to an embassy of one of these nations asking the government to let Christians worship Jesus; this can be in their own words.
•Ensure the letter is posted.
•Pray for a persecuted nation. |
| **And Finally!** | •Sing a praise song and thank Jesus for the time together. |

Parents or Discipleship Time	•Use the *Living With Jesus – Talking & Listening* workbook for children No. 3 – Checking It Out!

This week!	•Pray for the children to have a vision for the nations of the world to know Jesus. •Pray over the letters you sent to embassies that with a child like voice they will make a difference. •Ensure that the letters to the embassies are posted.

No. 4 – Knowing His Voice

Items You Will Need	•Refreshments; music for the worship time; objects for the worship time; large piece of material or a bed sheet; pictures you have previously used of unreached people; persecuted nations and nations you have prayed for; "Listening To Jesus" notebooks; pencils

Welcoming Each Other	•During this time have a drink and a snack. Clear away before beginning icebreaker. •As the children come in, encourage them to share about their week and you share about yours. Ensure that every child has the opportunity to share while everyone shows respect for the person speaking.
Icebreaker	•Hold up a large piece of material and ask half the group to go on one side and the rest to go to the other so that they can't see each other. •One child after the other should say the word "Jesus"; the other group must guess whose voice it is! They are allowed to disguise their voices. •Repeat the experience, but this time do NOT allow them to disguise their voices.

Worshipping Jesus	**Theme: Everything Can Remind You Of Jesus** •Bring in a series of objects and hand one to each person. •Ask them how this reminds them of Jesus. Examples: flower – I am more precious to Jesus than a flower; cup – I can be empty like this cup for Jesus to fill us; phone – Jesus will always answer me; etc. •Ask each person to pray about how they were reminded of Jesus. •Stand in a circle. Have each person turn to the right, with each of them putting their hands on the shoulders of the one in front of them. Pray for that person. •Turn around and do the same for the person who had prayed for you.

Jesus' Word and Your Lives	**Theme: Recognizing The Shepherd's Voice** •Talk about the icebreaker time. How could they recognize voices? How easy was it? Could they have recognized the voice of a stranger? Ask which voices they recognized the easiest. Point out that the more they know someone, the better they will recognize the voice. •Read John 10:2-4. •Spend some time talking about this: Who is the shepherd, what kind of shepherd is He, why do the sheep follow Him, who are His sheep, etc.?

(continued)

<table>
<tr><td></td><td>

•Encourage the children to share times when they have found it difficult to listen to Jesus' voice and then when they have found it easy to listen to Him. Allow plenty of time for this and pray for each other as appropriate.
•Encourage them that the more they listen to Him the easier they will know His voice, just as was discussed at the beginning.

</td></tr>
</table>

Memory Verse Experience	•Ask several children to read John 10:3. •Give the children their notebooks, and let them write the verse in it. •Ask each person, including yourself, to write, "Speak my Shepherd, I am listening," and then to write what they believe they hear from Jesus. •Share these together. Check out that everyone agrees that what has been heard is in line with the Bible. •Repeat John 10:3.

Witnessing for Jesus	**Theme: The Nations** •Read Psalm 2:8. "I will make the nations your inheritance, the ends of the earth your possession." •Talk about the unreached people, the persecuted nations and nations you have prayed for. Bring in pictures you have previously used to help. •Go into two groups. One prays for unreached people, and the other for people who are persecuted in prison or hurt for Jesus. Then change over! •Remind them that Jesus is counting on their generation to go and reach these nations.
And Finally!	•Spend a few moments thanking Jesus for all the fun He will bring this week.

Parents or Discipleship Time	•Use the *Living With Jesus – Talking & Listening* workbook for children No. 4 – Knowing His Voice!

This week!	•Pray that each child will spend time listening to the Holy Spirit this week.

No. 5 – Being With Jesus

Items You Will Need	• Refreshments; worship music; a chair; globe; "Listening To Jesus" notebooks, pencils

Welcoming Each Other	• During this time have a drink and a snack. Clear away before beginning icebreaker. • As the children come in, encourage them to share about their week and you share about yours. Ensure that every child has the opportunity to share while everyone shows respect for the person speaking.
Icebreaker	• "If someone was going to give you a special surprise, what would you like it to be and why?"

Worshipping Jesus	**Theme: Jesus In The Center** • Place one chair in the middle of the circle. • Ask the group to imagine Jesus sitting in the empty chair. • Ask them to share what Jesus might say to them if He was sitting there. • Quietly sing a worship song to Him. • Thank Him that He is with you all. • Sing a praise song.

Jesus' Word and Your Lives	**Theme: Spending Time With Jesus** • Ask the children how they think they can please Jesus and make Him really happy. Notice how many of the responses will be "doing" rather than "being." • Tell the story of Mary and Martha (Luke 10:38-42). Dramatize Martha rushing around getting everything ready while Mary sits and listens to Jesus. Ask the children what they think about Martha and what they think about Mary in that situation. Help them to understand what both of them were trying to achieve. • Read Luke 10:38-42 and ask the children what Jesus appreciated most and ask them why. • Now share with one another the things that stop you from spending time quietly listening to Jesus. Talk about how you can make sure that you give Jesus all the time and attention that He loves to have with you. • Talk together about the things that Jesus might have wanted to talk with Martha and Mary about. • What are the things that He loves to spend time talking with you about? (continued)

	•Imagine that you are all sitting with Jesus. What might He say to you? Write it in your notebooks. •Share this together. Ask the children if this checks out with the Bible as each person reads what they have written, at the same time affirming them in what they have written. Pray about anything that may arise during this time.

Memory Verse Experience	•Ask several of the children to read 1 John 5:11. •Share together what this might mean. •Go around the circle with one person saying, "God has given us eternal life," and the next saying, "and this life is in His Son." At the end, have everyone say 1 John 5:11 in unison. •Do this several times.

Witnessing for Jesus	**Theme: The Nations** •Read Psalm 2:8. "I will make the nations your inheritance, the ends of the earth your possession." •Show them a globe and spend a few moments looking at the many nations. •Read Matthew 28:18-20 and ask them what they think Jesus means when He says you are to "go." He tells you to go to "all nations", and He has given you His authority to go. •Put the globe in the middle and ask the children to read Matthew 28:18-20 as they lay hands on it. •Spend a few moments in quiet looking at the globe. Ask them to listen to Jesus as they do this. •Share together what everyone believed they heard Jesus say and respond appropriately by praying, etc. •Read Psalm 2:8 again!
And Finally!	•Sing a praise song and thank Jesus for your time together.

Parents or Discipleship Time	•Use the *Living With Jesus – Talking & Listening* workbook for children No. 5 – Being With Jesus

This week!	•Pray that each child will not only hear the call for laborers for the harvest field of the world, but will respond.

No. 1 – Love For Me & Love For Others

Items You Will Need	• Refreshments; paper and pencils to make an invitation for Jesus, *"Listening to Jesus"* notebooks; pencils; spare chairs; quiet worship music

Welcoming Each Other	• During this time have a drink and a snack. Clear away before beginning icebreaker. • As the children come in, encourage them to share about their week and you share about yours. Ensure that every child has the opportunity to share while everyone shows respect for the person speaking.
Icebreaker	• "Share one thing you are good at and one thing you find difficult."

Worshipping Jesus	**Theme: What Is Heaven Like?** • Spend some time talking about what you all think heaven will be like. Don't let them just give spiritual answers – include things like fun, exciting. etc. • Read Revelation 21:3-5. • What does it tell you about heaven? • Sing a song about heaven/going to be with Jesus/Jesus leaving heaven. • Thank Jesus for preparing heaven for you.

Jesus' Word and Your Lives	**Theme: Why Did Jesus Come?** • Discuss together why you think Jesus left all that He had in heaven to come to earth. What did He have on earth and what did He have in heaven? • Read John 3:16 and share what you think it meant for the Father to "send" Jesus. • Write an invitation to Jesus to come to earth. Tell Him what the earth would be like for Him. The group could do this in twos or threes: e.g. "Dear Jesus, I want to invite you to a world that will kill you, where they won't listen to you, and will throw you out of the town where you lived…" • Do you think that you would have accepted an invite like that? • Spend a few moments thanking Jesus for coming. • Spend some time considering how you react to people who are unkind. • Put on some quiet music, give every child their *"Listening to Jesus"* notebook and let them ask Jesus "Why did you come to earth for me?" • Share your responses. Do they check out against the Word?

| **Memory Verse Experience** | *Who did Jesus come for? Everyone!
•Read John 3:16 several times. "Everyone who believes in Him may have eternal life."
•Share what this means to you.
•Jesus came so everyone could be His friend. |

| **Witnessing for Jesus** | **Theme: Praying For Those Who Are Lost To Know Jesus**
•Name two people you are praying for who don't know Jesus.
•Go around the circle putting that person's name into the Scripture e.g. "…who believes in Him may have eternal life."
•Each of you make a space or get an empty chair for one person you are praying for who does not yet know Jesus. Lay your hands on that chair and pray, pray, pray for that person to believe in Jesus. |
| **And Finally!** | •Kneel together and sing a quiet worship song. Pray! |

| **Parents or Discipleship Time** | •Use the *Living With Jesus – Love For Me & Love For Others* workbook for children No. 1 Love For Me & Love For Others |

| **This week!** | •Place an empty chair in your home. Pray over it daily for the salvation of all those children who are being prayed for by the children in your group. |

No. 2 – The Enemy

Items You Will Need	•Refreshments; *"Listening To Jesus"* notebooks; blindfolds - 1 per child; labels; obstacles, worship music, markers

Welcoming Each Other	•During this time have a drink and a snack. Clear away before beginning icebreaker. •As the children come in, encourage them to share about their week and you share about yours. Ensure that every child has the opportunity to share while everyone shows respect for the person speaking.
Icebreaker	•"Tell the group one thing about yourself that you think no one there knows."

Worshipping Jesus	**Theme: Do You Know What You Are Singing?** •Sing a song the children really know well. •Encourage them to sing it again – this time tell them to really think about what they are singing. •Share together what you noticed the second time as you sang it. •Pray about anything that is said. •Sing the song again encouraging the children to think about the words.

Jesus' Word and Your Lives	**Theme: How Does The Enemy Keep You From Seeing Jesus?** •Blindfold one child and put a few obstacles in their way. Ask them to find their way through the obstacles to "Jesus." Repeat this with several (or all) of the children, changing the obstacles slightly each time a different child is blindfolded. •Ask one of the children to go through the obstacles to "Jesus" without a blindfold. Ask why the second was easier? (No blindfold!) •Discuss the fact that people (their friends included) cannot see the way to Jesus because they are "blindfolded." They are in darkness. What things does Satan use as his blindfold? e.g. bad videos; things other people say; wrong music; peer pressure. •Take the blindfold and put labels on it with their suggestions. •Read 1 John 5:19 and share what it means to each of you. •Discuss how you can help people to see their way to Jesus: e.g. knowing the Bible so you can share it with them; praying for them; serving them; letting them see Jesus in you.

<table>
<tr><td>Memory Verse Experience</td><td>

- Read Revelation 22:12 together, "Behold I am coming soon!"
- "Who is He coming for?" Everyone who believes in Him.
- Stand up and repeat Rev 22:12 going around the circle while each person says, "Behold Jesus is coming soon for…" (put a name of someone who believes in Jesus.) Do this several times.
</td></tr>
</table>

<table>
<tr><td>Witnessing for Jesus</td><td>

Theme: Opening The Eyes Of Those Who Don't Know Jesus
- Give each child a blindfold and ask them to put labels on it naming the things that are stopping their friends from seeing Jesus.
- Put all the blindfolds on the floor; kneel in front of your own.
- Remove each label from the blindfold one at a time. For each label, pray that Jesus will remove the blindfold from their friends' eyes so they will be able to see Him.
- Repeat this until every label has been destroyed.
</td></tr>
<tr><td>And Finally!</td><td>

- Sing a praise song about Jesus setting you free. Pray.
</td></tr>
</table>

<table>
<tr><td>Parents or Discipleship Time</td><td>

- Use the *Living With Jesus – Love For Me & Love For Others* workbook for children   No. 2 – The Enemy
</td></tr>
</table>

<table>
<tr><td>This week!</td><td>

- Place a blindfold in your house and pray over it every day that the eyes of a generation of children and young people will be opened to see Jesus.
</td></tr>
</table>

No. 3 – Standing In The Gap

Items You Will Need	• Refreshments; *"Listening to Jesus"* notebooks; paper; pencils; something to make two lines on the floor; large sheet of paper with the name "Jesus" written on it; smaller pieces of paper; music for the worship time

Welcoming Each Other	• During this time have a drink and a snack. Clear away before beginning icebreaker. • As the children come in, encourage them to share about their week and you share about yours. Ensure that every child has the opportunity to share while everyone shows respect for the person speaking.
Icebreaker	• "If you could be any animal, which one would you be, and why?"

Worshipping Jesus	**Theme: Worship From The Heart** • Choose a worship song and notice if the children are really thinking about what they are singing (see last week!!). • Ask them to share what was happening in their hearts as they sang. • Sing another worship song kneeling down and ask them to respond in their hearts as they sing. • Go around the circle asking each person to pray from his or her heart.

Jesus' Word and Your Lives	**Theme: Standing In The Gap** • Ask the children to stand behind two lines opposite one another that are too far apart for any child to jump the GAP. • Tell the children they have to get from one side to Jesus who is standing on the other side of the GAP, without touching the floor between the lines. • When they fail to do this, ask them to get into pairs and say that now one of the two must get across the GAP without touching the floor. They may carry their partner, etc. • Discuss the difference between the two; what changes in attitude they had; how they helped each other across the GAP to Jesus. • Read Ezekiel 22:30. Discuss the verse together. God was looking for a man who would help rescue the nation. He could find no one! What did it mean for the land that no one was prepared to help the nation back to God? • He is looking for people who will stand in the gap and bring their friends to Him. (continued)

	• Discuss how we can help friends across the gap to bring them to Jesus: e.g. pray; tell them; bring them to the small group meeting; let them see Jesus in us. • Ask the children to stand if they want to volunteer to Jesus to stand in the gap for their friends. • These children (and adults) should lift up their hands and offer themselves to Jesus. • Clap that Jesus now has volunteers…He has found someone today.

Memory Verse Experience	• John 13:34. Discuss what this means in your families: e.g. how can you live this verse at home, how does Jesus love you. • Ask the children to get into pairs, learn the verse together and find a way of miming what it says so the message is heard without words. • Share this! • Say the verse together.

Witnessing for Jesus	**Theme: Helping Friends To "Cross The Gap"** • Write the names of friends who don't know Jesus on pieces of paper. • Lay these on the floor away from the paper labeled "Jesus." • Pick up a paper and slowly walk with it praying all the time for that person until you lay it on the "Jesus" paper. • Repeat this until every name has been prayed for and taken across the gap!
And Finally!	• Stand around the sheet with the papers and the name of Jesus. • Sing a praise song. • Pray for yourselves and the children who need Jesus for the coming week.

Parents or Discipleship Time	• Use the *Living With Jesus – Love For Me & Love For Others* workbook for children No. 3 – Standing In The Gap

This week!	• Pray for the parents of the children in your small group. • Call the parents and ask for prayer requests.

No. 4 – Love Without Limits

Items You Will Need	• Refreshments; *"Listening to Jesus"* notebooks; pencils; map of your country; quiet music

Welcoming Each Other	• During this time have a drink and a snack. Clear away before beginning icebreaker.
	• As the children come in, encourage them to share about their week and you share about yours. Ensure that every child has the opportunity to share while everyone shows respect for the person speaking.
Icebreaker	• "Describe one incident when someone, other than your parents, showed by their actions that they loved you."

Worshipping Jesus	**Theme: What Are You Singing?** • Choose a praise song and ask some of the children to say the words. • Talk about which parts mean a lot to you and why. • Sing the praise song. • In pairs, pray for each other. • While still in pairs, sing a worship song, perhaps kneeling together and holding hands.

Jesus' Word and Your Lives	**Theme: Jesus' Unconditional Love** • Ask the children to get into pairs and see if there is anything they think would make Jesus love them more. • Discuss this together, "Jesus loves you just as you are." He will never love you more. He will never love you less. • Why do you think that Jesus' love is different from the way you love? • Read together James 2:1-4. Act it out and talk about what it says. • Think of examples of when you have been nicer to one person than to another. Share these examples together. • Now take one of those examples and say what Jesus would have done in that situation. • Pray prayers of repentance for not having the love for others that Jesus has for them. Ask Him to fill you with His love. • Play some quiet music; ask Jesus to talk to you about His love. • Share with one another what you thought Jesus said. Check that you all think this agrees with the Bible.

<table>
<tr><td>Memory Verse Experience</td><td>

- Read Ezekiel 22:30. "I looked for a man who would build up the wall and stand in the gap on behalf of the land."
- Say the verse together. Remember what was shared last week and what you think the verse means.
- Put a map of your country on the floor and talk about why your country needs Jesus.
- Lay your hands on the map and everyone pray for two minutes for your country.
</td></tr>
</table>

<table>
<tr><td>Witnessing for Jesus</td><td>

Theme: Prayer Walking
- Find the place on the map where you live.
- Why does your town/city need Jesus? How much does He love your town/city?
- Go and stand by a door or a window and pray for the place where you live.
</td></tr>
<tr><td>And Finally!</td><td>

- Sing about the love of Jesus. Pray that this week His love will go through you to others.
</td></tr>
</table>

<table>
<tr><td>Parents or Discipleship Time</td><td>

- Use the *Living With Jesus – Love For Me & Love For Others* workbook for children No. 4 – Love Without Limits
</td></tr>
</table>

<table>
<tr><td>This week!</td><td>

- Pray for the parents of the children in your small group. How many of the homes do you visit regularly?
</td></tr>
</table>

No. 5 – Agape Love

Items You Will Need	• Refreshments; a paper with the word "agape" written on it; a scroll for each child; colored pencils; worship music

Welcoming Each Other	• During this time have a drink and a snack. Clear away before beginning icebreaker. • As the children come in, encourage them to share about their week and you share about yours. Ensure that every child has the opportunity to share while everyone shows respect for the person speaking.
Icebreaker	• "If you could meet anyone in the world, who would you like to meet and why would you like to meet them?"

Worshipping Jesus	**Theme: Tell Jesus You Love Him** • Sing a song about the love of Jesus. • Share together how you know He loves you. • Ask who needs to know Jesus' love in a very special way. Ask them to sit on a chair in the middle and have everyone lay hands on them praying that they come to know the love of Jesus in a special way. • Sing another song about Jesus' love.

Jesus' Word and Your Lives	**Theme: Jesus' Unconditional Love (Agape)** • Talk about last week's meeting and how Jesus loves everyone unconditionally. • Read Romans 5:8. "While we were sinners, Christ died for us." Talk about what this means to you, go into detail about what it cost Jesus and how He could have made different decisions about the cross if He had not loved you so much. • Show the children the word "AGAPE" and explain that is a very special love…the love you have been talking about this week and last week. Read Romans 5:8 again – this is agape love. • Write your own small group "poem." Go around the group asking each person to complete the line, "I know Jesus loves me because…" Write each statement and then read it out loud together. • Ask the children if there are times when they wonder if Jesus does love them. Allow them to share and allow other children to minister to them. • Pray for any child who shared with the group.

<table>
<tr><td>Memory Verse Experience</td><td>

- Read together, "Keep the royal law found in Scripture. Love your neighbor as yourself." James 2:8
- Talk about the importance of obeying a "royal law"!
- Give each child a scroll that they can write the verse on and color it so it looks like a royal decree.
- Stand and hold the scrolls, open them together, and read the Scripture as if declaring a "royal decree"!

</td></tr>
</table>

<table>
<tr><td>Witnessing for Jesus</td><td>

Theme: Equipping To Share A Personal Testimony
- Go around the group and ask a few of them to share why they are following Jesus. They should pretend that they are sharing with someone who does not know much about Him. The leader should do this first, making it very simple, short and emphasizing "why" you are following Jesus today. (You will continue this over the next two weeks with the rest of the group. This will encourage and equip them to share with the unsaved.)

</td></tr>
<tr><td>And Finally!</td><td>

- Sing a song about the love of Jesus. Pray together.

</td></tr>
</table>

<table>
<tr><td>Parents or Discipleship Time</td><td>

- Use the *Living With Jesus – Love For Me & Love For Others* workbook for children No. 5 – Agape Love

</td></tr>
</table>

<table>
<tr><td>This week!</td><td>

- Examine your own heart in relation to agape love and each of the children in your group. Pray for a fresh flow of love for each one.

</td></tr>
</table>

No. 6 – Building Them Up

Items You Will Need	• Refreshments; heart shape; container; quiet music; cards; music; pencils

Welcoming Each Other	• During this time have a drink and a snack. Clear away before beginning icebreaker. • As the children come in, encourage them to share about their week and you share about yours. Ensure that every child has the opportunity to share while everyone shows respect for the person speaking.
Icebreaker	• "If you could change one thing in your home, what would it be and why?"

Worshipping Jesus	**Theme: Expression Of Love To Jesus** • Sing a worship song. • Give each child a cut out heart shape. • Play quiet music and ask each child to write on the card why they love Jesus so much. • Sing another worship song as they hold their "heart" to Jesus. • Place the hearts in a container and thank Jesus for His wonderful love.

Jesus' Word and Your Lives	**Theme: Helping Others When They Need "Building Up"** • Share together times when you felt unhappy and someone helped you feel better. What would it have been like if no one had been there to help? Did it please you to have their help and support? How did they help you? Etc. • Read Romans 15:2, "Each of us should please his neighbor for his good, to build him up." Build up could mean "encourage." • Did the people who helped you do what this verse says? • Think of someone you know who is feeling "down" and needs to be "built up." What could you say that would help? • Give each child a card to write to someone who they think needs to be encouraged. • Put some quiet music on and tell each child to ask Jesus what He would like to say to that person. Write it on the card. • When everyone is ready, hold the cards in your hands and pray for that person. • Make sure that all the cards will be delivered to the person they have been written to.

<table>
<tr><td>Memory Verse Experience</td><td>• Ask a child to read Romans 5:8, "While we were still sinners Christ died for us."
• Then discuss what this verse means to you (see last week).
• Ask the children to repeat the verse changing the word "we" and "us": e.g. "While I was still a sinner…" "While (insert a name) was still a sinner…"
• Ask a child to thank Jesus for dying for all of you.</td></tr>
</table>

<table>
<tr><td>Witnessing for Jesus</td><td>Theme: Equipping To Share A Personal Testimony
• Continue to go around the group and ask a few of them share why they are following Jesus. They should pretend that they are sharing with some one who does not know much about Him. (You will continue this over the next week with the rest of the group. This will encourage and equip them to share with the unsaved.)</td></tr>
<tr><td>And Finally!</td><td>• In pairs, pray for each other and the coming week.</td></tr>
</table>

<table>
<tr><td>Parents or Discipleship Time</td><td>• Use the Living With Jesus – Love For Me & Love For Others workbook for children No. 6 – Building Them Up</td></tr>
</table>

<table>
<tr><td>This week!</td><td>• Pray for the parents of the children in your small group. How many of the homes do you visit regularly?</td></tr>
</table>

No. 7 – Running The Race

Items You Will Need	• Refreshments; quiet music; a line on the floor and call it the finish line; a crown on the line; a large sheet of paper with "our lives" on it; counters; a cup; some small sweets; "Listening To Jesus" notebooks; pencils

Welcoming Each Other	• During this time have a drink and a snack. Clear away before beginning icebreaker. • As the children come in, encourage them to share about their week and you share about yours. Ensure that every child has the opportunity to share while everyone shows respect for the person speaking.
Icebreaker	• "What have you done that was the most fun in the last week or two?"

Worshipping Jesus	**Theme: What Is Worship** • Ask the children what they think "worship" is. (One child said, "It is when I want to take Jesus out of my heart and give Him a kiss.") • Help the children to understand worship is about their hearts and not just what they do during "worship." • Ask the children to be quiet as you play some music and ask them to see what is in their hearts towards Jesus. • Share together and pray for each other to really have hearts that are full of worship to Him. • Sing a worship song.

Jesus' Word and Your Lives	**Theme: Finishing The Race!** • Share what happened when the cards were given to people who needed encouragement last week. • Talk together about races you have seen or taken part in. Share with one another whether you enjoyed races or not, what the prizes were, etc. • Ask several children to read Acts 20:24. "If only I may finish the race and complete the task Jesus has given me." Then, share what it means to you. • Cover the following points: your lives are a race; you can all be winners; you can all receive a prize; Jesus will give the prizes out; He has a task for each of you to do; and it is not a race to be first, but a race to run well. • Place a line on the floor and call it the finish line. Put a crown on the line, place a large sheet of paper in front of the line and write "our lives" on it. Explain this set up to the group.

(continued)

	• Give everyone a pencil and ask them to write the things we can do for Jesus (the task: tell others about Him) and the qualities in our lives that will make us winners in the race towards Jesus: e.g. love; faithfulness. • Discuss running a race for Jesus and how that compares with earthly races: e.g. the prize will last forever; everyone can be a winner; being with Jesus is the greatest prize of all. • Ask the group if there is anything they struggle with in the race for Jesus. Listen to them and then pray for them by asking them to go into the middle of the group and have everyone lay hands on them.

Memory Verse Experience	• Ask several children to read Acts 20:24. "If only I may finish the race and complete the task the Lord Jesus has given me." • Ask the group to write the verse in their *"Listening to Jesus"* notebook. • Put on some quiet music and ask the Holy Spirit to give you a picture about the race that you are in with Jesus. • Share your pictures together. • Pray each child's picture. • Repeat Acts 20:24 together.

Witnessing for Jesus	**Theme: Equipping To Share A Personal Testimony** • Finish going around the group asking the rest of the children to share why they are following Jesus. (They should pretend that they are sharing with someone who does not know much about Him.)
And Finally!	• Give three cheers for Jesus and thank Him for the prize he is getting ready for you.

Parents or Discipleship Time	• Use the *Living With Jesus – Love For Me & Love For Others* workbook for children No. 7 – Running The Race • *No. 8 – Looking Back and Going On* is not a small group week. It is a time for each child to be able to identify breakthroughs that they still need, and to spend some time with Jesus. This requires quality time with each child.

This week!	• If the parents are not doing *Living with Jesus* with any child – set aside time with each child to do *No. 8 "Looking Back and Going On."* This is vital for their discipleship.

No. 1 – The Soul

<table>
<tr><td>Items You Will Need</td><td>•Refreshments; assorted sweets; paper for each child with "I think… I feel… I choose to…" written on them; large sheet of paper; large sheet with the SOUL rhyme on it (see Word section); markers; pencils; worship music; set a date and make some preparations for a fun time 5 weeks from now; create one invitation for each child so they can invite an unsaved friend</td></tr>
</table>

<table>
<tr><td>Welcoming Each Other</td><td>•During this time have a drink and a snack. Clear away before beginning icebreaker.
•As the children come in, encourage them to share about their week and you share about yours. Ensure that every child has the opportunity to share while everyone shows respect for the person speaking.</td></tr>
<tr><td>Icebreaker</td><td>•"If you could make one rule in your home, what would it be and why would you make it?"</td></tr>
</table>

<table>
<tr><td>Worshipping Jesus</td><td>Theme: Worship In The Psalms
•Choose about 6 lines from Psalm 136:1-9. Read it asking the children to say "His love lasts forever" after each line.
•Ask the children to share what their favorite line was and why it was special to them.
•Sing about the love of Jesus.
•Ask each person to pray thanking Jesus for some way that He has shown His love to them.</td></tr>
</table>

<table>
<tr><td>Jesus' Word and Your Lives</td><td>Theme: Understanding The Soul
•Give each child a paper with "I think… I feel… I choose to…"
•Put sweets in the centre circle so the children can see them.
•Be very quiet and look at the sweets – after a few moments ask each child to complete "I think …"! (I would like one, that piece is my favorite, etc).
•Discuss their thoughts and tell them "the MIND is where you THINK" (write this for the children to see).
•Remove the sweets and put them away.
•Stay quiet and then ask the children to complete "I feel …" about the sweets being taken away (disappointed, angry, upset, etc).
•Discuss their feelings and point out that "EMOTIONS are where you FEEL" (write this on the large sheet of paper).

 (continued) </td></tr>
</table>

	• Show the sweets again, ask the children to look at them and choose what they would like to do. Complete "I choose to…"!
	• Discuss their choices and point out that "your WILL is where you CHOOSE." (Write this on the large sheet of paper.)
	• Discuss their choices and allow them to do what they choose! (Presumably to eat one!!)
	• Now tell them that the WILL + EMOTIONS + MIND are the SOUL. Talk about this so they understand.
	• Everyone read, learn, and say the following SOUL rhyme: "I THINK in my MIND – I have so many thoughts. I FEEL with my EMOTIONS – happiness, sadness, peace and fear. I CHOOSE with my WILL – to help, to be lazy, to play or to work. MIND, EMOTIONS, and WILL are my SOUL! MIND, EMOTIONS, and WILL are my SOUL!"
	• Repeat this leaving out different CAPITALIZED words and see if they can remember them.
	• Discuss that your soul (mind, will and emotions) are all to praise Jesus. Your minds will think as Jesus' mind, your will choose as Jesus chooses, your emotions will feel as Jesus feels.
	• Ask each child to pray for either their mind, will or emotions to be like Jesus (let them choose according to their own need).

Memory Verse Experience	• Ask three of the children to read Psalm 146:1-2. "Praise the Lord O my soul. I will praise the Lord all of my life."
	• Give the children one minute in silence and see which child can repeat it without looking at it.
	• Repeat it all together.

Witnessing for Jesus	**Theme: Planning A Small Group Outreach – Choosing A Friend**
	• Tell the group that together you are going to plan a party for each of them so they can bring a friend who does not know Jesus.
	• Tell them the date.
	• Ask them for ideas for the get-together.
	• Pray about which friend to invite and write the name down on a party invitation.
	• Each person should hold their invitation and pray for that child.
	• Keep the invitations. (Do not let the children pass them out yet. You'll bring them back to the group for the next couple of weeks.)
And Finally!	• Hold hands in a circle and have everyone pray for the person on the left and then for the person on the right.

| **Parents or Discipleship Time** | • Use the *Living With Jesus – Strongholds* workbook for children No. 1 – The Soul |

| **This week!** | • Strongholds are difficult concepts for some children; pray that they will understand as they begin the journey to identify strongholds in their lives. |
| | • Inform the parents about the planned Fun Day when the children will invite their unsaved friends. |

No. 2 – Having A Stronghold

Items You Will Need	•Refreshments; an item stuck together so it cannot be separated; the rap from the Word section written out; label of either "mind", "will" or "emotions"; invitations from last week; markers, large sheet of paper

Welcoming Each Other	•During this time have a drink and a snack. Clear away before beginning icebreaker. •As the children come in, encourage them to share about their week and you share about yours. Ensure that every child has the opportunity to share while everyone shows respect for the person speaking.
Icebreaker	•"Who is the strongest person you know, how do you know they are strong?"

Worshipping Jesus	**Theme: Worship In The Psalms** •Read Psalm 100 several times, going around the group reading a verse each. •Talk about how many ways you can praise Jesus in this Psalm. •Read verse 2. Stand and sing a song of praise, with glad and joyful hearts. •Read "Enter his courts with thanksgiving" verse 4. •Spend some time kneeling and thanking Him for being your God, your Savior, your King, etc.

Jesus' Word and Your Lives	**Theme: Having A Stronghold** •Show the children something that is stuck together so strongly that they cannot part it. Ask them to try and separate it. •Discuss things that have a hold on your lives that you find hard to get off: e.g. lying, stealing, bullying, laziness. When a suggestion is given say, "Yes, that can hold on strongly to us." •Have a large sheet of paper and draw a circle called the Kingdom of God. Put some qualities of the kingdom in the middle: e.g. kindness, truth, honesty. •In another color, put things that invade God's Kingdom just like an enemy does: e.g. unkindness, dishonesty, laziness. These are called "strongholds" because they hold onto you strongly! •Who can get rid of these – weapons that Jesus gives you like the Bible. Read 2 Corinthians 10:4 together. •Then say the following rap and have fun with it: *Whatever has a stronghold it must go, go, go!* *Whatever holds me strongly, it must GO?* *When Jesus goes to war – then Satan can be sure* *That whatever holds on strongly it must GO!*

| **Memory Verse Experience** | • Ask three people to read 2 Corinthians 10:4.
• Talk about what this means to you.
• Go into pairs and put actions to the verse. Each pair should show the group and then ask the group to copy them as they repeat the verse. |

| **Witnessing for Jesus** | **Theme: Planning A Small Group Outreach – Praying For Friends**
• Talk about the Fun Day you will be having and get ideas from the children.
• Give them some responsibilities for that day.
• Hand out the invitations. Have the children pair up and exchange invitations. While holding the invite, have them pray for each other's friend who will be coming.
• Place all the invites in the middle and lay hands on all of them and have everyone pray at once for those who will be coming. |
| **And Finally!** | • Hold hands in a circle and thank Jesus for the freedom you have. |

| **Parents or Discipleship Time** | • Use the *Living With Jesus – Strongholds* workbook for children No.2 – Having A Stronghold |

| **This week!** | • Fast and pray for one day this week as you lead the children into freedom from things that are controlling their lives. |

No. 3 – Rejoicing Souls

Items You Will Need	• Refreshments; 2 chairs; paper and pencils; paper and envelopes; large sheet of paper and marker; worship music; invitations from the previous weeks

Welcoming Each Other	• During this time have a drink and a snack. Clear away before beginning icebreaker. • As the children come in, encourage them to share about their week and you share about yours. Ensure that every child has the opportunity to share while everyone shows respect for the person speaking.
Icebreaker	• "What time would you say was the happiest time of your life, and why?"

Worshipping Jesus	**Theme: Worship In The Psalms** • Read Psalm 100 again this week with each person taking a verse. • Ask which one is their favorite verse and why. • Read verse 4. Make a "gate" with two chairs for everyone to walk through. Place a container one side of the "gate." • Ask everyone to write some things that they are thankful for on a piece of paper. • Let each one take a turn to walk through the "gate" to the container and place their paper in it saying "I am thankful for…" • Read verse 4 again together. • Sing a song of thanksgiving as you all walk through the "gate."

Jesus' Word and Your Lives	**Theme: Rejoicing Souls** • Go over some of the things you have talked about the past two sessions: i.e. the WILL + EMOTIONS + MIND are the SOUL. The mind is where you think, the emotions are where you feel and the will is where you choose. A stronghold is something that holds onto you very strongly like lying, etc. Give as much time to this as necessary to ensure that everyone understands. • On the large piece of paper draw a circle with "mind - thoughts" in it. Ask everyone to write some good thoughts to go in the circle: e.g. "I will be kind, I will help". • Draw another overlapping circle with "will - choices" in it and ask everyone to write some good choices they could make in the circle: e.g. I could choose to help my parents, I could choose to obey. • Draw a third overlapping circle with "emotions – feelings" in it and ask everyone to write some good feelings in it: e.g. love, peace.

(continued)

	• Now draw one big circle to encompass all three and write "The Soul" explaining that all these together make up the soul. (Keep this for the next session.) • Read Isaiah 61:10. "I delight greatly in the Lord, my soul rejoices in my God." Talk about what this person's soul was doing: e.g. being happy, excited about God. • Ask everyone to be really quiet and ask if what they are thinking makes Jesus happy, if the things they are choosing make Jesus happy, if the things they are feeling make Jesus happy. Take these one at a time and give the children time to consider a response. • Give everyone a time to pray and respond to the time of quiet.
Memory Verse Experience	• Read Isaiah 61:10. "I delight greatly in the Lord; my soul rejoices in my God." • Read it again emphasizing "I" and "my." • Repeat it with "you" and point to another person. • Ask the children to repeat the verse in the same way that you did!
Witnessing for Jesus **And Finally!**	**Theme: Planning A Small Group Outreach – Praying For Friends** • Share the update about the Fun Day, being sure to pick up on any ideas that the children have which would be appropriate. • Pray in pairs for yourselves (e.g. your responsibilities, that you would really be Jesus to the other children, etc.). • Then stand in a circle and pray for the whole day. • Hand out the invitations. Ask the children to kneel with their invite. Have them ask Jesus if there is anything He would like to say to them about the child they are inviting. Share these responses together. • Pray over the invites and let the children take them to give out. • Pray for boldness this week for each child in your group.
Parents or Discipleship Time	• Use the *Living With Jesus – Strongholds* workbook for children No. 3 – Rejoicing Souls
This week!	• Continue to pray that each child will understand what the Holy Spirit is saying to them about their soul. • Pray for each child being invited to the Fun Day.

No. 4 – The Enemy

<table>
<tr><td>Items You Will Need</td><td>•Refreshments; large sheet of paper; markers; music for the worship time; "The Soul" paper from last week</td></tr>
</table>

<table>
<tr><td>Welcoming Each Other

Icebreaker</td><td>•During this time have a drink and a snack. Clear away before beginning icebreaker.
•As the children come in, encourage them to share about their week and you share about yours. Ensure that every child has the opportunity to share while everyone shows respect for the person speaking.

•"If you could change one thing about yourself what would it be and why?"</td></tr>
</table>

<table>
<tr><td>Worshipping Jesus</td><td>Theme: Worship In The Psalms
•Read Psalm 148:1-4 several times together.
•Go round the circle and see how many things in these verses praise Jesus.
•Now make your own Psalm listing things everyone can think of that praises Jesus: e.g. "Praise Him all children, Praise Him beautiful mountains, Praise Him…"
•Stand and read your own Psalm together as worship to Jesus.
•Sing a praise song.</td></tr>
</table>

<table>
<tr><td>Jesus' Word and Your Lives</td><td>Theme: Understanding The Enemy's Tactics
•Show the paper from the last session with the soul and ask the children to explain it to you. (This helps you to know if they have understood.)
•Focus on the circle with "mind - thoughts" in it. Now ask everyone to write in a different color some bad thoughts they could think of: e.g. "I will be unkind, I will steal."
•Repeat this in the circle with "will - choices" in it and ask everyone to write some bad choices they could choose: e.g. I choose to gossip, I choose to disobey."
•Repeat this in the circle with "emotions – feelings" in it. Ask everyone to write some bad feelings: e.g. jealousy, hate.
•Remind the children of the memory verse last session (Isaiah 61:10) and ask if these things are a way to delight in God.
•Explain that these things can hold you very strongly and remind them that you then call them strongholds – it is Jesus who can remove them from your lives.
•Ask someone to read Psalm 38:22 explaining that Jesus is just waiting for you to ask Him to help you with these strongholds.
•Spend some time thanking Jesus that he is bigger, stronger and more powerful than anything that can hold you.</td></tr>
</table>

| **Memory Verse Experience** | • Read Psalm 121:2. "My help comes from the Lord, the Maker of heaven and earth."
• Explain that this verse shows the power of Jesus; He really is greater than everything.
• Divide the group into two: one side asks, "Who can help you?" and the other says the memory verse; then change. |

| **Witnessing for Jesus** | **Theme: Planning A Small Group Outreach –**
Being Jesus To Their Friends
• Encourage the children to share what happened when the invitations were given out. Pray as necessary.
• Spend some time with any practical preparations for the Fun Day.
• Talk about what it would look like for you to "be Jesus" to your friends: e.g. fun, kind forgiving, etc.
• Ask the children to share areas that they might find difficult about "being Jesus": e.g. letting other children go first, not taking the largest piece of cake.
• Pray for each other that Jesus will be seen in you. |
| **And Finally!** | • Hold hands in a circle sing an appropriate song and pray for the coming week. |

| **Parents or Discipleship Time** | • Use the *Living With Jesus – Strongholds* workbook for children No. 4 – The Enemy |

| **This week!** | • Remember to pray for each member of your small group daily.
• Continue to pray into and plan the Fun Day, and encourage the full involvement of the parents. |

No. 5 – Down With Strongholds

Items You Will Need	Refreshments; large sheet of paper and marker; labels with "mind", "will" and "emotion" (enough for each group to have one label per child)

Welcoming Each Other	• During this time have a drink and a snack. Clear away before beginning icebreaker. • As the children come in, encourage them to share about their week and you share about yours. Ensure that every child has the opportunity to share while everyone shows respect for the person speaking.
Icebreaker	• "If you could invite someone to be a part of your family, who would it be and why?"

Worshipping Jesus	**Theme: Worship In The Psalms** • Read Psalm 145:1-4 several times. • Talk about this together – what don't they understand, what impacts them, etc. • Verse 2 says, "every day I will praise you." • Take a large sheet of paper and write down each day of the week. • Spend a while thinking back through the week of things that you can praise Jesus for in each of your lives. Write these under each day. • Ask if each person thanked Jesus when these things happened – it's so easy to forget to thank Him. • Sing a song of thanks to Jesus as you stand around the paper. • Spend some time kneeling around the paper, and thanking Jesus for all the ways He cares for you.

Jesus' Word and Your Lives	**Theme: Down With Strongholds** • Put the children into groups of three and then give each child a label of either "mind", "will" and "emotions." • Tell each group that they are a soul that follows Jesus. Ask each group of three to make a sequence: e.g. the mind - I will help; the will - I choose to help; the emotions - I feel happy that I am going to help. • Repeat the above with each group making a sequence of a soul that does not follow Jesus: e.g. I will steal a sweet; I choose to steal a sweet; I feel greedy for that sweet. • Share with the children about repentance… that it is not only being sorry, but also changing.

(continued)

<table>
<tr><td></td><td>

- Ask them to talk about ways the souls that did not follow Jesus could repent and change.
- Read 1 John 4:4. "The One who is in you is greater than the one who is in the world." Explain that Jesus is greater than all the things that have a stronghold on you.
- Play some quiet instrumental music and ask the children to spend some time with Jesus asking Him to set them free of the things that have a stronghold on them.
- Pray together, "Lord Jesus, I know that you are greater than the things that hold me so strongly. I ask you by the power of your Holy Spirit to drive this out of my life. Thank you for doing this for me…"
- Give the children an opportunity to share what they asked Jesus to do for them.

</td></tr>
</table>

Memory Verse Experience	• 1 John 4:4. "The One who is in you is greater than the one who is in the world." • Repeat this together a few times and each time you read it make the sign of victory.

Witnessing for Jesus	**Theme: Planning A Small Group Outreach – Final Details** • Ask the children how their friends responded when given the invite. Pray as necessary. • Check out the details of the Fun Day, ensuring that the children have ownership of it. • Stand in a circle and pray for the Fun Day. Ask the children to suggest areas that you should pray for.
And Finally!	• Stand and hold hands thanking Jesus for all He did to give you victory.

Parents or Discipleship Time	• Use the *Living With Jesus – Strongholds* workbook for children No. 5 – Down With Strongholds

This week!	• Pray daily for the victory gained in these young lives to take root. • Have the Fun Day…. And enjoy it! Remember to follow up with all the children who were invited and continue to pray for them.

What Do You Choose?

No. 1 – Choosing To Be Happy

<table>
<tr><td>Items You Will Need</td><td>•Refreshments; large thank you card (made specially); pictures of different places of the city you live in; worship music</td></tr>
</table>

<table>
<tr><td>Welcoming Each Other</td><td>•During this time have a drink and a snack. Clear away before beginning icebreaker.
•As the children come in, encourage them to share about their week and you share about yours. Ensure that every child has the opportunity to share while everyone shows respect for the person speaking.</td></tr>
<tr><td>Icebreaker</td><td>•"If you could choose one thing to do tomorrow, what would it be and why?"</td></tr>
</table>

<table>
<tr><td>Worshipping Jesus</td><td>Theme: The Presence Of Jesus
•Ask how many are present? Have you included Jesus?
•Welcome the presence of Jesus as you stand in a circle.
•Sing a song that focuses on Jesus as you stand.
•Ask each child for a word describing Jesus: e.g. fantastic, fun.
•Then repeat, saying "Jesus, you are…(e.g. great)."
•Give Jesus a clap!</td></tr>
</table>

<table>
<tr><td>Jesus' Word and Your Lives</td><td>Theme: Choosing To Be Happy
•Ask everyone to share something that made them really happy.
•Ask if they would be unhappy without the experience they shared.
•Ask if anyone has been really happy without something special happening… just being happy.
•Discuss whether it is possible to be happy just because of Jesus. Remind them that some people have no homes, no money, and no toys and are happy because they have Jesus.
•Read Psalm 126:2. Imagine what great things made these people so happy.
•Consider what Jesus has done for you and ask whether that makes you happy or if you rely on other things for happiness.
•Make a big "Thank you card" for Jesus. Everyone fill it with what Jesus has done to give you laughter and joy.
•Sing a praise song around the card and thank Jesus with joy!</td></tr>
</table>

<table>
<tr><td>Memory Verse Experience</td><td>

• "The Lord has done great things for us and we are filled with joy." Psalm 126:3.
• Ask every person to repeat this but personalize it by filling in the blank: "The Lord has… and I am filled with joy".
• Then repeat the verse from the Bible.

</td></tr>
</table>

<table>
<tr><td>Witnessing for Jesus</td><td>

Theme: The Place Where You Live
• Show the children pictures of the neighborhood where you live. Can they identify the places? What do they know about them?
• Ask who these places belong to. Finally discuss the fact that they belong to Jesus.
• Put the pictures on different chairs, divide the children into groups so they can rotate and each group pray over every picture.

</td></tr>
<tr><td>And Finally!</td><td>

• Ask everyone to kneel, spending a few moments asking Jesus to fill them with His love so it overflows to everyone they meet.

</td></tr>
</table>

<table>
<tr><td>Parents or Discipleship Time</td><td>

• Use the *Living With Jesus – What Do You Choose?* workbook for children No. 1 – Choosing To Be Happy

</td></tr>
</table>

<table>
<tr><td>This week!</td><td>

• Pray for each child that they will live only for Jesus.

</td></tr>
</table>

What Do You Choose?

No. 2 – Happiness & You

<table>
<tr><td>Items You Will Need</td><td>• Refreshments; music for worship</td></tr>
</table>

<table>
<tr><td>Welcoming Each Other</td><td>• During this time have a drink and a snack. Clear away before beginning icebreaker.
• As the children come in, encourage them to share about their week and you share about yours. Ensure that every child has the opportunity to share while everyone shows respect for the person speaking.</td></tr>
<tr><td>Icebreaker</td><td>• "If you could learn to play any instrument what would it be and why?"</td></tr>
</table>

<table>
<tr><td>Worshipping Jesus</td><td>Theme: Praising With Instruments
• Read Psalm 150:3 – 6.
• Talk about this together – and discuss instruments that you might use to worship Jesus both at home and in your church.
• Play an instrumental track of music so the children can hear an instrument being used to praise Jesus.
• Play the track again and ask the children to close their eyes and spend some time just with Jesus – what He might say, what He might show, what they might like to say to Him.
• Share together and respond as appropriate.
• If you have an instrumental of a song the children know – use it to worship, showing how instruments help you praise Jesus – but it is what is in our hearts that really matters!
• Pray for the people who lead worship in your church.</td></tr>
</table>

<table>
<tr><td>Jesus' Word and Your Lives</td><td>Theme: Happiness Jesus' Way
• Make a list of things that people think make them happy.
• Read Matthew 5:1-12 and find the best children's version for this.
• Make a list beside the first one of the things Jesus said would make us happy: e.g. peacemakers, humble people, people who are want to live like Jesus, people who are kind and forgiving even when others are not, people who keep their heart pure, people who are mistreated because they follow Jesus.
• Consider some of these helping the children to understand that other things that make you happy don't last forever. The things Jesus spoke about make you happy because they are about your friendship with Him. They will last forever. They bring others to Jesus. (A whole different set of value - verse 12.)
• Each person identify which of these they find difficult. Talk about why this is so and pray for one another.</td></tr>
</table>

<table>
<tr><td>Memory Verse Experience</td><td>

•Read Psalm 150 and then ask if David was happy or sad when he wrote this. Discuss why David might have been so happy.
•Read verse 6. Why does David want to praise Jesus?
•Say this verse together several times emphasizing the word "everything."

</td></tr>
<tr><td>

Witnessing for Jesus

And Finally!

</td><td>

Theme: The Place Where You Live
•Ask the children to share about their schools – the problems and the good things.
•Ask the children from one school to stand in the middle, the rest of the group surround them and pray for their school. Repeat this until each school has been prayed for, including home schoolers.
•Join hands and pray for all schools in your area that the children and staff will meet Jesus.

•Ask the children to surround you and pray for you as leaders.

</td></tr>
<tr><td>Parents or Discipleship Time</td><td>

•Use the *Living With Jesus – What Do You Choose?* workbook for children No. 2 – Happiness & You

</td></tr>
<tr><td>This week!</td><td>

•Read Matthew 5:1-12 each day naming every child in your group.

</td></tr>
</table>

What Do You Choose?

No. 3 – Choosing To Obey

Items You Will Need	• Refreshments: strip of paper and markers for each child; worship music

Welcoming Each Other	• During this time have a drink and a snack. Clear away before beginning icebreaker. • As the children come in, encourage them to share about their week and you share about yours. Ensure that every child has the opportunity to share while everyone shows respect for the person speaking.
Icebreaker	• "What do you think will be the first thing you do and say when you meet Jesus in heaven and why?"

Worshipping Jesus	**Theme: Worshipping The King** • Sing about the greatness of Jesus. • Play instrumental music, and ask everyone to kneel and imagine Jesus on the throne in Heaven. • Give everyone the opportunity of speaking to Him. • Then ask if they know what Jesus is saying to them. • Sing a worship song as you close your eyes and sing to the King on the throne.

Jesus' Word and Your Lives	**Theme: Choosing To Obey** • Discuss whether you are happiest when you obey or disobey Jesus. • Now discuss the fact that if it is true you are happiest when you obey, why do you disobey Him so often? • Read Acts 5:15 -18 and 28 to find out why these people were put in prison and what it would have been like. • Then tell the children what the prisoners were told to do when they were released from prison in verse 28 (the first part only). • Ask the children to imagine if they had been in prison what they would have done. • Now read the whole story from verses 15-29 in a very dramatic way. • Ask the children to retell the story in their own words. • Show that Jesus took care of the prisoners for obeying Him and that their happiness was because they had obeyed Jesus. • Now share about times when it is difficult to obey Jesus and pray for one another.

<table>
<tr>
<td>Memory Verse Experience</td>
<td>

• Ask different children to read Acts 5:29. "We must obey God rather than men."
• Talk about the fact that you are told by Jesus to obey your parents and those He gives to care for you.
• Now say the verse in different ways: e.g. "We must obey God rather than…" e.g. the TV, your friends, stealing, lying, etc.
• Repeat the verse together; then say "I will obey, etc".

</td>
</tr>
</table>

<table>
<tr>
<td>Witnessing for Jesus</td>
<td>

Theme: The Place Where You Live
• Give each child a piece of paper so they can write the name of their street on it.
• Ask them to write the names of everyone they know on their street.
• Share what has been written to gain an understanding of the streets where they live. Then ask them to stand in the middle and hold up their paper and pray.
• Finally hold up your street and let them pray for you.

</td>
</tr>
<tr>
<td>And Finally!</td>
<td>

• Stand in a circle, walk in that circle and imagine that you are walking your street. Pray that your feet will be Jesus' feet every step you take this week.

</td>
</tr>
</table>

<table>
<tr>
<td>Parents or Discipleship Time</td>
<td>

• Use the *Living With Jesus –What Do You Choose?* workbook for children No. 3 – Choosing To Obey

</td>
</tr>
</table>

<table>
<tr>
<td>This week!</td>
<td>

• Pray for wisdom that comes from Jesus as the children live in obedience to Jesus.

</td>
</tr>
</table>

No. 4 – Choosing To Forgive

Items You Will Need	Refreshments; worship music; picture/brochure about your workplace

Welcoming Each Other	• During this time have a drink and a snack. Clear away before beginning icebreaker. • As the children come in, encourage them to share about their week and you share about yours. Ensure that every child has the opportunity to share while everyone shows respect for the person speaking.
Icebreaker	• "The Children: If you could give your leader one gift, what would it be and why?" • The Leader: if you could give the children one gift, what would it be and why?

Worshipping Jesus	**Theme: Jesus Is Here!** • Start by making a point of welcoming each child and telling them how glad you are that they are present. • Then ask if you forgot to welcome anyone (Jesus!). • Ask one of the children to welcome Jesus. • Sing a praise song. • Ask if anyone needs prayer: e.g. for healing, because they are unhappy, etc. Ask them to stand in the middle while the group lays their hands on them as different people pray. • Sing a worship song.

Jesus' Word and Your Lives	**Theme: Making The Holy Spirit Happy** • Talk whether you really care if you make others unhappy. Discuss some of the things you might change if you did care: e.g. you would not retaliate, not gossip, etc. • Who do you make unhappy sometimes? e.g. family, friends. • Read and talk about Ephesians 4:30. "Do not grieve the Holy Spirit of God." How do you do this? Do you care if you upset Him? • Ask the children to go into threes and act out a time when one person has been treated unfairly. Then show these examples. • Now ask them to go back into their groups and act out what should happen to please the Holy Spirit and what would happen that would upset Him. Show these examples to each other. • Encourage honesty in sharing what each person might have done in any of these situations.

Memory Verse Experience	•Read and say Ephesians 4:32 out loud. "Be kind, forgiving each other as in Christ God forgave you." •Discuss how much Jesus forgives you and if you really forgive and show kindness to each other like that. •Say the verse again. •Spend some time repenting for the times that each person has made the Holy Spirit unhappy and asking Him to remind you each time you are in danger of hurting Him.

Witnessing for Jesus	**Theme: The Place Where You Live** •Share with the children about your workplace (or ask another adult to come and share). If possible, bring a picture or brochure about it. •Tell them about the difficulties and the joys you face there. Let the children ask questions. •Give the children some specific prayer requests for your workplace and ask them to lay hands on whoever is sharing and pray.
And Finally!	•Stand together and say, "Holy Spirit we want to spend this week making you happy." Pray over this!

Parents or Discipleship Time	•Use the *Living With Jesus – What Do You Choose?* workbook for children No. 4 – Choosing To Forgive

This week!	•Pray for a spirit of forgiveness to be seen in the children's lives so that bitterness does not take root in them as they grow.

What Do You Choose?

No. 5 – Choosing Who Controls You

Items You Will Need	• Refreshments; small pieces of paper; string; markers; something to attach the paper to the string; prayer requests from the leader of your church; worship music; paper, pencil and envelope for each child

Welcoming Each Other	• During this time have a drink and a snack. Clear away before beginning icebreaker. • As the children come in, encourage them to share about their week and you share about yours. Ensure that every child has the opportunity to share while everyone shows respect for the person speaking.
Icebreaker	• "If you could be any age, how old would you like to be and why?"

Worshipping Jesus	**Theme: A Gift For Jesus** • Welcome the presence of Jesus as you stand. • Sing about Jesus. • Ask each person "If you could give Jesus a gift right now, what would it be and why?" Listen carefully and respond as appropriate. • Talk about why the best gift is your lives. • Give the opportunity to thank Jesus that he is your greatest gift. • Sing a worship song together.

Jesus' Word and Your Lives	**Theme: Who Is Controlling You?** • Talk about the different ways things are controlled: e.g. switches, remote controls, steering wheels. • Now discuss ways that you are controlled: e.g. you are told what to do, you decide, you listen to others. • Read Matthew 26:69-75 and talk about why Peter said he did not know Jesus: e.g. fear. • What sometimes controls you and causes you to make decisions: e.g. fear, popularity, pleasing others. Talk about times when this has happened. Give examples from your own life too. • Discuss the fact that Satan is behind all these. • Give each child a piece of paper with a string attached to put their name on. • Ask them to put paper on the string naming some of the negative things that control them.

(continued)

	• Now show them they are controlled by these things because Satan pulls that string. • Repeat this putting Godly characteristics on the string: e.g. boldness, kindness, forgiveness – Jesus is in control! • Ask each child one negative and one positive thing from the string. Then tell them to ask Jesus to remove the negative and repent from letting it have control. Then ask for the positive. • Finally, take all the negative things, tear them up and put them in a container to be thrown away!!! That is what Jesus does!

Memory Verse Experience	• Jesus loves you so much that His love can remove anything from your lives. • Read 1 John 3:1. "How great is the love the Father has lavished on us, that we should be called the children of God." • Discuss what lavished means. Discuss other people who "lavish" love on you and show how much more Jesus does this. • Put the children into groups of three and give each group one minute to learn the verse. Then hear each group say it!

Witnessing for Jesus	**Theme: The Place Where You Live** • Let the children share about the Church you attend… who do they know, what do they see, etc. (This will give you their perspective!) • Share with them the prayer requests that you have from the leader of your church and inspire them that their prayers matter. • Pray for the requests. Ask the children if they hear anything from Jesus for the church. • Ask each child to write a letter to the leader saying they prayed for them and what they believe Jesus is saying to the church. • Place these in an envelope and arrange some time for the children to go with you to take the letters to the leader.
And Finally!	• Stand together and lay hands on the envelope and pray for your leader.

Parents or Discipleship Time	• Use the *Living With Jesus – What Do You Choose?* workbook for children No. 5 – Choosing Who Controls You

This week!	• Pray that each child would walk in uncompromising holiness.

No. 1 – What Is Faith?

Items You Will Need	•Refreshments; large sheet of paper; quiet instrumental music; paper and pencil for each child; worship music

Welcoming Each Other	•During this time have a drink and a snack. Clear away before beginning icebreaker. •As the children come in, encourage them to share about their week and you share about yours. Ensure that every child has the opportunity to share while everyone shows respect for the person speaking.
Icebreaker	•"Name one thing you would like to do if you had the chance. Why would you like to do it?"

Worshipping Jesus	**Theme: Precious To Jesus** •Sing about the love of Jesus. •Ask several children to read Matthew 6:26. •Ask the children to share what it means to them. •As you play some quiet instrumental music, ask the children to write down what Jesus tells them about His love for them. •Sing another song about His love. •Play the music again without singing and ask the children to close their eyes, hold up their hands and receive Jesus' special love for them. •Quietly close in prayer.

Jesus' Word and Your Lives	**Theme: What Is Faith?** •Blindfold a child and ask them some questions that shows they believe in something even if they can't actually see it: e.g. Do you believe that the sky is still there? Are you certain that there are trees outside? •Ask the group some questions that show you live by faith all the time: e.g. How did you know that the chair you are sitting on would hold you? Will you get any presents for Christmas? When you came into the building did you worry about it falling down? •Tell them that this is faith. Faith believes when you don't see what you believe: e.g. You will get Christmas presents even if you don't see them. You will have something to eat when you get home! •Ask the group if they can think of any other things they believe in that they haven't seen: e.g. Another country exists, there are planets in the universe.

(continued)

- Ask the group to read Hebrews 11:1. "Now faith is being sure of what we hope for and certain of what we do not see." Talk together about this.
- Ask the group who they know in the Bible who believed something they could not see: e.g. Mary knew she would give birth to the Son of God. Abraham knew he would have a son when he was very, very old. The disciples believed in Jesus so they followed Him. Paul knew Jesus was coming again.
- Ask the group what things the Bible says that they find hard to believe.
- Repeat that it is not possible to explain these things. "We believe it even if we can't see it."
- Pray for those who have doubts and problems in the area of believing when they can't see.

Memory Verse Experience	<ul><li>Say Hebrews 11:1. "Now faith is being sure of what we hope for and certain of what we do not see."</li><li>Ask the group for an example of something they hope for and are certain will happen: e.g. Christmas presents!</li><li>Ask them, "Are you sure that Jesus came to live and die for you? That is faith!" Give other examples by asking the question about being sure and being certain.</li><li>Repeat together Hebrews 11:1.</li></ul>

Witnessing for Jesus

Theme: Praying for the Music Industry
- Ask the children which singers they know and which music they like…make a list.
- Ask them how many of these groups/singers/bands know Jesus. Hopefully, you will end up with a mixture of Christian and non-Christian musicians.
- Ask them what problems they think these people will face.
- Point out how these people are able to influence others and how Jesus loves them.
- Let each person choose a name on the paper, lay hands on that name and pray for them.

And Finally!
- Thank Jesus for being with you!

Parents or Discipleship Time
- Use the *Living With Jesus – Having Faith* workbook for children No. 1 – Having Faith

This week!
- Look for opportunities to connect with the children and their unsaved friends outside the context of the meeting.

Having Faith

No. 2 – Faith Without Seeing, Feeling Or Touching

Items You Will Need	• Refreshments; Hebrews 11:1 written as individual words on separate pieces of paper; worship music, brochure of one the schools, paper, pencil and envelope for each child; sticky tape; large ball

Welcoming Each Other	• During this time have a drink and a snack. Clear away before beginning icebreaker. • As the children come in, encourage them to share about their week and you share about yours. Ensure that every child has the opportunity to share while everyone shows respect for the person speaking.
Icebreaker	• "If you could be really good at one thing you can't already do, what would that be and why?"

Worshipping Jesus	**Theme: Precious to Jesus** • Sing about the love of Jesus. • Ask different children to read Jer. 33:3, "I have loved you with an everlasting love." • Spend some time talking about what this means. • Pray about anything that has been discussed. • Sing again about the love of Jesus. • Play the song again without singing. In pairs, lay hands on one another asking for the love of Jesus to flow over the other person. • Now sing the song again.

Jesus' Word and Your Lives	**Theme: What Is Faith?** • Spend a few moments letting the children recall last week's meeting. • Ask one of the children to read Hebrews 11:1. • Remind them that faith is "I'll believe it even if I can't see it!" • Read Acts 3:1-5 and let each child end the story telling what they think they would have done if they had met the lame man. • Then read Acts 3:1-10 in a version that will help you make the story dramatic for the children. • Read it again asking three of the children to mime it as you read. • Discuss why you think Peter had faith to believe this man would walk: e.g. He had lived with Jesus; he had received the Holy Spirit; he knew the power of God had raised Jesus from the dead, so it could heal this man.

(continued)

	• Discuss what you think the lame man could have thought as he was asked to get up and walk! e.g. Peter was crazy; he was being made fun of. • Then talk about why they think the lame man did as Peter asked him. (He had faith!) • Share times when you have had faith. (Come prepared with examples!) • Ask the children to share times when they have had faith for something. • Spend some time thanking Jesus for all that He has given you in the Bible and in your lives to show you that you can trust Him even when you can't see the answer.

Memory Verse Experience	• Repeat the verse as it is foundational to the series on faith. • Take the words of Hebrews 11:1 and mix them up. See if any child can work out what they say: "Now faith is being sure of what we hope for and certain of what we do not see." • Repeat it, changing words: e.g. "Faith is being a little sure…"; "Faith is being sure we will get what we dream for…". Ask the children to correct you if you make a mistake.

Witnessing for Jesus	**Theme: Praying for Sports Personalities** • Ask the children which sports they play and how much they enjoy that sport. • Ask them to name famous people who play sports. Talk about how well known they are and what their lives must be like. • Ask the question, "Does Jesus love them more, or less than each of us because they are famous!" (He loves us all the same.) • Give each person a piece of paper. Ask them to write down the name of the sport and the person they would like to pray for. • Stick the papers on a ball. • Stand in a circle and take turns gently throwing the ball around the circle. Whoever has the ball must pray for someone whose name is on the ball!
And Finally!	• Thank Jesus for being with you and for His love for the people you just prayed for!

Parents or Discipleship Time	• Use the *Living With Jesus – Having Faith* workbook for children No. 2 – Faith Without Seeing, Feeling or Touching

This week!	• Continue to look for opportunities to connect with the children and their unsaved friends outside the context of the meeting.

No. 3 – What About Other People?

Items You Will Need	• Refreshments; globe or map; paper to write down prayer requests; extra chairs; worship music, blindfold, large thank you card; pictures of leading politicians with their names clearly printed on them

Welcoming Each Other	• During this time have a drink and a snack. Clear away before beginning icebreaker. • As the children come in, encourage them to share about their week and you share about yours. Ensure that every child has the opportunity to share while everyone shows respect for the person speaking.
Icebreaker	• "If you could change your name, what would you like to be called and why?"

Worshipping Jesus	**Theme: Precious To Jesus** • Read John 3:16. "God so loved the world that He gave…" • You all know how this verse ends – but discuss what you might put if you did not know the ending. • What does this show about the love of God for you? • Sing about the love of Jesus. • Stand around a globe/map and sing a song about the love Jesus has for the world. • Lay your hands on the globe/map and pray for the love of Jesus to reach all the nations.

Jesus' Word and Your Lives	**Theme: Faith With Action!** • Ask a child to stand facing away from you. Stand behind them and ask them to fall back into your arms. • Do they have the faith to fall? Try with several children. • Then try again, but blindfold the child first. • Ask them why this is more difficult. Remind them that faith is, "I'll believe it even if I can't see it." • Tell the children the following story, "There was a man who could walk on a tight rope very high up. One day he decided to try something really hard. He tied the rope to one side of Niagara Falls and then to the other. He then walked right across! People were watching, so he went to one of the men and said, "Do you believe that I could carry you on my back across the water fall?"

(continued)

- Ask the children what they would have answered.
- Tell them the man answered that he did believe it.
- Then ask them whether they thought he got on the tightrope walker's back to go across. Ask those who said, "Yes," whether they would have gotten on his back.
- The man refused to get on!
- The man said he believed, but he did not get on the back of the tightrope walker! Talk about the fact that the man said he believed, but he did not act. What does that mean? e.g. He did not really believe.
- Ask a child to read James 2:26, "Faith without works is dead," and ask what the verse has to do with the story! (You only really have faith and believe things if you DO them).
- Does the group have any examples of things they say they believe, but won't actually do? (Come with your own example.)

Memory Verse Experience	• Place a chair in the middle of the group. Ask them individually if they believe the chair will hold them if they sit on it. • Each one should say, "Of course, I do," and then sit on it, saying, "Faith without works is dead." James 2: 26.

Witnessing for Jesus	**Theme: Praying for your Government** • Take the pictures of those who are leading your country and ask the children if they recognize any of the people and what they know about them. Fill in any details yourself. • Stress the important task these people have and tell the children about one or two decisions they have had to make recently. • Ask some of the children to hold the pictures. Tell them that the Bible says we should "pray for those in authority over us." Then ask the other children to go to one of the pictures, lay hands on it and pray for that person. • Repeat this several times.
And Finally!	• Thank Jesus for being a friend you can always trust and have faith in!

Parents or Discipleship Time	• Use the *Living With Jesus – Having Faith* workbook for children No. 3 – What About Other People?

This week!	• Continue to look for opportunities to connect with the children and their unsaved friends outside the context of the meeting. This is essential in helping them to see that importance of reaching their friends for Jesus. It shows that you value their friends, too. • Ensure the card gets delivered this week.

No. 4 – Believing That You Are Special

Items You Will Need	• Refreshments; paper; pencils; poster board; worship music; large thank you card; pictures of leaders of other countries with their name and country clearly printed on each picture (the internet will help)

Welcoming Each Other	• During this time have a drink and a snack. Clear away before beginning icebreaker. • As the children come in, encourage them to share about their week and you share about yours. Ensure that every child has the opportunity to share while everyone shows respect for the person speaking.
Icebreaker	• "If you could wear anything you liked for a day, what would you wear and why?

Worshipping Jesus	**Theme: Jesus Is Precious To His Children** • Welcome the presence of Jesus. • Sing a song that focuses on the name of Jesus. • Give each person some paper and ask him or her to write down some words that they think describe Jesus. Encourage them to use words that they use every day, like fantastic! • Put all these papers on the floor and kneel around them. • Go around saying "Jesus, we think you are…" until every descriptive word has been used. • Put all the papers on a board headed "Jesus is…" (Keep this board for next week). • Sing the song again that you sang at the beginning.

Jesus' Word and Your Lives	**Theme:Believing That You Are Very Special** • Spend some time discussing why you think Jesus loves you. • Ask the children if they think that Jesus loves them more when they are good than when they do wrong things. Encourage the children to think about it carefully and to be really honest about it. Many children believe that love is based on performance. • Tell the children a story about a time when you felt that Jesus might love you less, and how you know His love did not change. • Remind the children of the story of when Peter denied Jesus (Matthew 26:69-74). • How do you think Peter felt when he saw Jesus again? What do you think He thought about how much Jesus loved him now?

(continued)

<table>
<tr><td></td><td>

- Now read John 21:15-20 and ask the children what happened when Jesus met him again: e.g. He ate with him; He talked with him; He gave Peter the chance to tell Him how much he loved Jesus; He spent time with him; He loved Him; He gave Peter special responsibilities for the church.
- Encourage the children to be honest about when they might struggle with receiving Jesus' love. Pray for each other to always know they are special to Jesus.

</td></tr>
</table>

Memory Verse Experience	• Read Joshua 1:5, " I will be with you; I will never leave you." • Encourage the children to personalize this by each one of them adding their ending to "Jesus will be with me and will never leave me even when…" • Repeat Joshua 1:5, "I will be with you, I will never leave you."

Witnessing for Jesus	**Theme: Praying for Another Government** • Take the pictures of leaders of other countries and ask the children if they recognize any of the people. • Explain who they are and go into detail about one of them: e.g. who they are; what country they lead; and how it differs from the country you are in. • Stand in a circle holding hands. Pray together for that nation and for the person who leads that nation.
And Finally!	• Thank Jesus for being with you.

Parents or Discipleship Time	• Use the *Living With Jesus – Having Faith* workbook for children No. 4 – Believing That You Are Special

This week!	• Continue to look for opportunities to connect with the children and their unsaved friends outside the context of the meeting. • Ensure the card is delivered this week

No. 5 – Keeping Your Faith

Items You Will Need	• Refreshments; worship music; 2 chairs; pencils; card; "Jesus is…" board from last week; picture of a prison or prison officer; paper

Welcoming Each Other	• During this time have a drink and a snack. Clear away before beginning icebreaker. • As the children come in, encourage them to share about their week and you share about yours. Ensure that every child has the opportunity to share while everyone shows respect for the person speaking.
Icebreaker	• "What task do you hate being asked to do and why?"

Worshipping Jesus	**Theme: Jesus Is Precious To His Children** • Stand and welcome the presence of Jesus. • Sing a song that focuses on Jesus very specifically. • Show the board "Jesus is…" from last week. • Ask each person to choose one that best expresses who Jesus is to them. • Ask each person why he or she chose that specific description. • Pray, "Thank you, Jesus, for being…" e.g. fantastic. • Stand and sing again about Jesus.

Jesus' Word and Your Lives	**Theme: Keeping Your Faith** • Ask a child to sit on a chair. • Then ask another child to sit on another chair and tell them that it has just been repaired and you are not sure if it will break. (This would not actually be true – the chair should be fine!) • Discuss together the difference between the way the two children sat on the chairs and why they reacted differently. • Discuss which child had more faith to sit on the chair and why. • "What stops you from having faith?" e.g. what other people say; the things you watch; what you think. • Read John 20:24-25 and talk about what was happening to Thomas' faith and why. • Read verses 26-28 together. • Discuss why you think Jesus said verse 27 to Peter. How did He know about Thomas faith? • Discuss whether Thomas had the faith that says, "I'll believe it, even if I don't see it."

(continued)

	• Read verse 29 and talk about what you believe Jesus meant. • At this point, act the story of John 20:24 -29. • Ask the children to share times when they don't believe things about Jesus because they cannot see heaven. Help them to understand that they can believe it because of faith. • Pray for each other.

Memory Verse Experience	• Say together John 20:29. "Because you have seen me you have believed; blessed are those who have not seen and yet have believed." • Divide the children into 2 groups. • Ask one half to say John 20:29 "Because you have seen me you have believed…" • Then the other half to say, "Blessed are those who have not seen and yet have believed". John 20:29. • Then change over. • Finally, say the whole verse together.

Witnessing for Jesus	**Theme: Pray for the Prison Service** • On a sheet of paper write the word "Prisoner. On another sheet of paper write the words "Prison Officer." • Ask the children what they think it might be like to be in prison for years. • Ask them what they think it would be like to look after people in prison. (Help them to have a picture that includes compassion and forgiveness.) • Ask them what things they think you should pray for (both for the prisoners and the prison staff). • Divide into two smaller groups. • Place one of the pieces of paper in the middle of each group. (If have a picture of a prison, or a prison officer this would be helpful.) • Ask the children to lay hands on the paper and pray. Then change papers and pray again. • Join in one circle and pray for the families of prisoners. Tell the children that boys and girls like them have parents in prison and how hard it must be.
And Finally!	• Ask two of the children to pray for the group as they go home and for their friends.

Parents or Discipleship Time	• Use the *Living With Jesus – Having Faith* workbook for children No. 5 – Keeping Your Faith

This week!	• Pray and fast for one day for all the children who have been prayed for and do not, as yet, know Jesus. • Ensure the card to the ambulance service is delivered.

No. 1 – Fighting in God's Army

Items You Will Need	• Refreshments; a cross; a heart; a nail; a flower; model soldiers or figures; music for worship

Welcoming Each Other	• During this time have a drink and a snack. Clear away before beginning icebreaker. • As the children come in, encourage them to share about their week and you share about yours. Ensure that every child has the opportunity to share while everyone shows respect for the person speaking.
Icebreaker	• "If you could create a new vehicle, what would it be like and why?"

Worshipping Jesus	**Theme: Reminding You of Jesus** • Place a cross, a heart, a nail, and a flower in the middle of the group. • Sing a praise song. • As you play some quiet music, ask everyone to look at the articles and choose one that speaks to them about Jesus. • Divide them into groups according to the article they chose. • Share in the groups why they chose it and pray. • Sing another praise song. • Ask for feedback about the time they spent in groups.

Jesus' Word and Your Lives	**Theme: Staying Together** • Spend some time talking about armies and how they work together to protect each other from the enemy. With some toy soldiers, or models, show how when one soldier goes off by himself, he is easily captured by the enemy. • Repeat this principle as you talk about sheep staying in the field with the other sheep and not wandering off alone. • Take this principle and show how you need each other so that Satan cannot harm you. • How does Satan try to pull you away from Jesus: e.g. listen to bad jokes, not attend our small group. • Talk about all the people God has put in your lives to help you stay protected: e.g. parents, teachers, your small group, pastor. • Read Hebrews 10:25, "Let us not give up meeting together." Ask why Paul wrote this. • Discuss how you can help each other to stay close to Jesus and not give Satan the opportunity of pulling you away. • Pray that you would care for and watch out for one another.

<table>
<tr><td>Memory Verse Experience</td><td>

- Read Hebrews 10:25, "Let us not give up meeting together…but let us encourage one another."
- Go around the group and say something encouraging to the person on your left. Give some time to think about this.
- Repeat the memory verse saying, "We will not give up meeting together…but we will encourage one another."
</td></tr>
</table>

<table>
<tr><td>Witnessing for Jesus</td><td>

Theme: Prayer Walking
- Tell the children you are going to prepare for a prayer walk.
- Ask what the children see as they walk down their streets: e.g. houses, people, cars.
- Now ask them to share what they think about when they see these things.
- Share that prayer is something you can do anywhere, at any time, and that Jesus is always listening to you, and wanting to talk with you.
- Ask them to close their eyes and imagine themselves walking down their street and praying for all the people who live there.
- Then discuss what difference that might make.
- Encourage them to start thinking about praying wherever they are and for whoever they see, especially on their own streets.
- Ask everyone to pray for the street where they live.
</td></tr>
<tr><td>And Finally!</td><td>

- Stand and pray for the street where you are meeting.
</td></tr>
</table>

<table>
<tr><td>Parents or Discipleship Time</td><td>

- Use the *Living With Jesus – Staying Protected* workbook for children No. 1 – Fighting in God's Army
</td></tr>
</table>

<table>
<tr><td>This week!</td><td>

- Pray safety and protection around each child as they face the temptations of their world.
</td></tr>
</table>

Staying Protected

No. 2 – Your Armor

Items You Will Need	• Refreshments; picture of scenery; worship music; pencil; paper

Welcoming Each Other	• During this time have a drink and a snack. Clear away before beginning icebreaker. • As the children come in, encourage them to share about their week and you share about yours. Ensure that every child has the opportunity to share while everyone shows respect for the person speaking.
Icebreaker	"What do you most appreciate about yourself and why?"

Worshipping Jesus	**Theme: Reminding You of Jesus** • Sing a worship song about the wonder of creation. • Show the group a picture of scenery. • Spend some quality time looking at the wonder of creation, ask the children to look at the details that no man could have done. • Read Genesis 1:20–23 asking what the children think as they hear it. • Lay hands on the picture and thank Jesus for all that He gave you. • Sing another song about creation.

Jesus' Words and Your Lives	**Theme: Your Armor** • Talk together about the armor soldiers wear to protect themselves: e.g. why they have it, what would happen without it. • Read Ephesians 6:17 and ask the children what they know about the armor of God. • Give every child paper and pencil. Read verses 14-17 very slowly. As you mention a piece of armor, let each child draw it. • Talk about what they drew and then ask if this is enough. • What happens if there is no commander of the army? • You need a commander for the army. Who is your commander? • Ask how Jesus leads His army of people: e.g. your group, family, church and talk about the importance of listening and obeying His commands. • Stand and hold hands praying that you would listen and obey Him as a group.

Memory Verse Experience	• Read Ephesians 6:17. "Take the helmet of salvation and the sword of the Spirit which is the Word of God." • Read it a second time asking the group to lift their Bibles when the "Word of God" is mentioned. • Discuss why the Bible is like a sword: e.g. because it sends Satan running, because it can show the truth by cutting through lies. • Repeat the verse together. • Conclude as you read 1 Timothy 1:17. "To the King who rules for ever, who will never die, who cannot be seen, the only God, be honor and glory for ever and ever. Amen."

Witnessing for Jesus	**Theme: Prayer Walking** • Ask the children if they remembered to pray for people in their street, and have their feedback. • Ask the children what they could pray for, especially when they don't know some of the people in their neighborhoods: e.g. to see Jesus, to meet people who will lead them to Jesus, for Jesus' love to touch them. • Go to the window and ensure that everyone can see. • As you look out, begin to pray for houses, people, cars, etc, helping the children if they need direction. • Remind everyone to pray for their own streets during the week.
And Finally!	• Return and join hands to pray for the streets where everyone lives.

Parents or Discipleship Time	• Use the *Living With Jesus – Staying Protected* workbook for children No. 2 – Your Armor

This week!	• Pray that each child and their parents that they will grow fully equipped with the armor of God.

No. 3 - Rescuing Others

Items You Will Need	• Refreshments; paper and pencil for each person; large sheet of paper; markers; worship music

Welcoming Each Other	During this time have a drink and a snack. Clear away before beginning icebreaker. As the children come in, encourage them to share about their week and you share about yours. Ensure that every child has the opportunity to share while everyone shows respect for the person speaking.
Icebreaker	• "If you could have one other person in this world as your friend who would it be and why?"

Worshipping Jesus	**Theme: Reminding You of Jesus** • Welcome the presence of Jesus as you stand together. • Read Genesis 1:26. "God said, 'Let us make man in our own image.'" Say that all people are wonderful and made by God. • Share that when you have Jesus in you and Jesus is in the other person then you see Jesus in each other. • Ask each person to share something beautiful they see in the person on their left. • In pairs, say "Jesus in me greets Jesus in you!" • Thank Jesus for each other. • Sing a worship song.

Jesus' Word and Your Lives	**Theme: Reaching Friends for Jesus** • Ask why you need an army. E.g. to protect, to rescue. • Discuss what the army of Jesus is for - to protect each other and to rescue others. • Talk about who needs rescuing: e.g. friends, family, nations. • Now talk about the things that might stop you from going to rescue people for Jesus: e.g. fear, being laughed at. • Read Luke 10:1-2 explaining you are His workers. Jesus knew there would not be enough workers so He asked you to pray for more people who would go and tell others about Him, no matter what it might cost them. • Give an opportunity for everyone to write down the things that stop them being bold for Jesus: e.g. shyness, laziness, fear. • Share that Jesus has said that He will be with you all the time so you are never alone in doing this.

Memory Verse Experience	•Read several times very slowly Romans 8:38-39. "I am convinced that neither death nor life, neither angels or demons, neither the present nor the future… will be able to separate us from the love of God." •Then go around the group and ask each person to repeat, "I am convinced that _______ will not be able to separate me from the Love of God." Give them the opportunity to personalize with things shared that prevent them from being bold. •Pray for each other to know God's love when it is difficult to tell others about Jesus.

Witnessing for Jesus	**Theme: Prayer Walking** •Get feedback from the children about praying for their own streets asking them what they prayed for. •Ask the children to tell you what sort of things Jesus does for people and write these on a large piece of paper: e.g. Jesus heals, Jesus provides, Jesus cares. •Envision the children to pray these things for people in homes they may never go into, e.g. I pray that this home would know Jesus as their healer, I pray that this home would know Jesus as their…." •Stand in the doorway where you are and watch the traffic going by. (Be sure no child can run out.) •Ask the children to watch for a car and call out "Jesus is your…" as it passes.
And finally!	•Stand and pray for your streets saying "Jesus is your…"

Parents or Discipleship Time	•Use the *Living With Jesus – Staying Protected* workbook for children No. 3 – Rescuing Others

This week!	•Think about each family of the children in your group and pray into their situation.

No. 4 – Who's In Charge?

<table>
<tr><td>Items You Will Need</td><td>• Refreshments; "Jesus" written in bold print; many small pieces of paper; pencils; responsible adults to help with the prayer walk; worship music</td></tr>
</table>

<table>
<tr><td>Welcoming Each Other</td><td>• During this time have a drink and a snack. Clear away before beginning icebreaker.
• As the children come in, encourage them to share about their week and you share about yours. Ensure that every child has the opportunity to share while everyone shows respect for the person speaking.</td></tr>
<tr><td>Icebreaker</td><td>• "What is the funniest thing that you can remember and why does it make you laugh?"</td></tr>
</table>

<table>
<tr><td>Worshipping Jesus</td><td>Theme: Reminding You of Jesus' Majesty
• Sing about Jesus.
• Ask everyone to share what they think Jesus looked like on the earth. (Help them to see that Jesus looked like any other child/man on the outside!)
• Now ask them what they think He looks like in heaven.
• Read Revelation 5:1-5 – let the children read it from different versions.
• Explain that you cannot understand or picture heaven, but this shows you how wonderful, powerful and fantastic Jesus is.
• Ask the children to close their eyes as you play quiet music and picture Jesus on the wonderful throne in heaven.
• Encourage everyone to say what they would like to say to Him as they "see" Him there.
• Kneel and sing a worship song about Jesus being King.</td></tr>
</table>

<table>
<tr><td>Jesus' Word and Your Lives</td><td>Theme: Nothing Between You and Jesus
• Ask everyone to write on pieces of paper and then share the things they think or talk about the most.
• Discuss why these things are so important to them.
• Talk with the children about the love that Jesus had for them – a love that meant He thought about them even before they were born, and then a love that meant He left everything to come and die for them.
• Read together John 3:16 and ask the children what it cost Jesus.
• Place the word "Jesus" in the center.
• Ask everyone to put the papers they wrote around the word "Jesus".
• As they look, they will see that these things are between them and "Jesus". Discuss how important they are compared with Jesus, and encourage honesty about whether they would want these things so much that they would put them before Jesus.</td></tr>
</table>

<table>
<tr><td>Memory Verse Experience</td><td>

• Read Romans 8:38-39.
• Reread the Scripture and ask different people to write the things that cannot separate you from the love of Jesus: e.g. death, life, angels.
• Place these with the papers the children wrote at the beginning around the word "Jesus" but leave space for everyone to stand in a circle between "Jesus" and the papers. Now these things cannot separate anyone from Him.
• Read Romans 8:38-39 together while standing in the circle.
• Encourage repentance for things that have come between them and Jesus and thank Him for His love that will always be there for them.

</td></tr>
</table>

<table>
<tr><td>Witnessing for Jesus</td><td>

Theme: Prayer Walking
• Divide the children into pairs with an adult (prayer triplets). Tell them you are going to go on a short walk and must hold hands. As they walk they will pray for homes, or any other places they pass. Give them an allocated length of time to be back.
• On returning have a brief feedback but tell them you will find out what happened next week

</td></tr>
<tr><td>And Finally!</td><td>

• Stand and pray together for the place where you are meeting and for the streets where everyone lives.

</td></tr>
</table>

<table>
<tr><td>Parents or Discipleship Time</td><td>

• Use the *Living With Jesus – Staying Protected* workbook for children No. 4 – Who's In Charge?

</td></tr>
</table>

<table>
<tr><td>This week!</td><td>

• Pray that Jesus would be the focus of every family represented by the children in your group.

</td></tr>
</table>

No. 5 – The Kingdom Will Last Forever

<table>
<tr><td>Items You Will Need</td><td>•Refreshments; 2 large sheets of paper; pencils; markers; worship music</td></tr>
</table>

<table>
<tr><td>Welcoming Each Other</td><td>•During this time have a drink and a snack. Clear away before beginning icebreaker.
•As the children come in, encourage them to share about their week and you share about yours. Ensure that every child has the opportunity to share while everyone shows respect for the person speaking.</td></tr>
<tr><td>Icebreaker</td><td>"Who is the person you would most like to say 'thank you' to and why?"</td></tr>
</table>

<table>
<tr><td>Worshipping Jesus</td><td>Theme: Reminding You to Say "Thank You"
•Sing a song giving thanks to Jesus.
•On a large sheet of paper, ask the group to write as many things as they can think of to thank Jesus for while the music plays.
•Stand and look at the paper – asking whether everything you can thank Jesus for is on the paper. (No!)
•Spend a few moments remembering you can never thank Him enough.
•Kneel around the paper and thank Him for some of these things.
•Sing another song of thanks.</td></tr>
</table>

<table>
<tr><td>Jesus' Word and Your Lives</td><td>Theme: The Kingdom of God
•Talk about the country you live in: e.g. what is it called, who rules it, some history about it.
•Explain that you are citizens of your country and talk about your flag, your national anthem, and your passport.
•Then talk about some people all over the world in different countries, all being citizens of another kingdom. Can they guess which kingdom it is? God's Kingdom.
•Read Luke 17:21. "The Kingdom of God is within you."
•You are in this kingdom because you have Jesus in you.
•Share ways this kingdom is different from the nation you live in: e.g. it goes across the world, it has a ruler and King who will never be replaced or die, anyone can join it.
•Depending on the ages of your children, either divide them into groups of three, or keep them altogether and make up an anthem for the Kingdom of God. (It can be recited or sung).
•Now make a flag for Jesus' kingdom.</td></tr>
</table>

Memory Verse Experience	• Read Daniel 2:44. "The God of heaven will set up a kingdom that will never be destroyed." • Stand with the flag of the Kingdom of God. Repeat the verse from Daniel several times. • Spend a short time thanking Jesus that you are part of the best Kingdom of all!

Witnessing for Jesus	**Theme: Prayer Walking** • Spend this time hearing about the previous week's prayer walks: e.g. where they went, what they prayed, what did Jesus tell them about the homes. • Ask each prayer triplet to stand while the others lay hands on them and pray for the places they went to. • Thank Jesus for hearing their prayers and for caring about every home they prayed for.
And Finally!	• Join hands and pray for parents and families that each child comes from.

Parents or Discipleship Time	• Use the *Living With Jesus – Staying Protected* workbook for children No. 5 – The Kingdom Will Last Forever

This week!	• Pray for the children's families to have wisdom and understanding.